DISCARD

The Beginning Filmmaker's Guide to Directing

The Beginning Filmmaker's Guide to Directing

Renée Harmon

Walker and Company
New York

791.43
HARMON
1993

First published in the United States of America in 1993
by Walker Publishing Company, Inc.

Published simultaneously in Canada by Thomas Allen & Son
Canada, Limited, Markham, Ontario

Library of Congress Cataloging-in-Publication Data
Harmon, Renée.
The beginning filmmaker's guide to directing / Renée Harmon.
p.   cm.
Includes bibliographical references and index.
ISBN 0-8027-1219-3. —ISBN 0-8027-7384-2 (pbk.)
1. Motion pictures—Production and direction.   I. Title.
PN1995.9.P7H37   1993
791.43'0233—dc20   92-5536
                                                          CIP

Book design by Claire Vaccaro
Printed in the United States of America
2   4   6   8   10   9   7   5   3   1

Ingram 11/27/92 2495/14.40

Contents

. . . .

Acknowledgments

I wish to thank Mary Kennan Herbert, at Walker and Company, for her interest in *The Beginning Filmmaker's Guide to Directing,* her belief in the book, and her encouragement.

I wish to thank Ed, my husband, and Cliff and Cheryl, my children, for their patience with me while the book was being written.

I wish to thank all the actors and crew who work with enthusiasm, tenacity, and diligence on my films, and the directors—most of all James Bryan, director, and Bill Luce, art director—who make the impossible possible.

I wish to thank the many aspiring filmmakers who, attending my lectures, provide me with insight as to what kind of information is valuable to them.

. . . . . .

Preface

We are witnessing a rapidly expanding motion picture market that, to be sure, provides product not only for the numerous multiple-screen theaters springing up all over the country, for cable, TV, and domestic video, but for the growing video market overseas as well. Consequently interest in film-making has never been stronger. You may be among the many talented, skilled artists who need only that one break to get a foothold in the motion picture industry. You may be ready to get a project off the ground and onto the screen.

The Beginning Filmmaker's Guide to Directing has been tailored to your specific needs. This book has been designed for you—the writer, actor, or cinematographer who wishes to enter the directing field. You have talent, vision, and tenacity; all you need are some commonsense, down-to-earth guidelines, some nuts-and-bolts advice to lead you in the right direction. You need the advice of a professional moviemaker, one who is actively engaged in producing and directing low-budget feature films.

This book has grown out of my own experiences as filmmaker and lecturer. I am familiar with the problems you—the beginning director with only limited funds at your disposal—will face.

So let's get to work. Pick up your slate, and . . . "Scene 1, Take 1."

Part One

Introduction

You—the writer, the actor, the cinematographer, the producer—own a motion picture script. You have something to say and *know* how it should be said. You have a mental image, and you know how it should be expressed. Almost physically you experience the mood of your script and the rhythm of its scenes. You are possessed by a vision demanding to come alive in the matrix seen on the screen. So you slave over a budget, you get investors, and if you are fortunate you'll arouse some distribution interest. You are ready to turn your vision into reality . . .

You sign a director. And all of a sudden, something strange and disturbing happens. The director, imposing his or her own vision onto the motion picture, turns it into a *project,* while the matrix you had envisioned and loved fades into the background. In front of your eyes, your film turns out very different from the one you had expected and battled for. This does not necessarily mean that the film is inferior to the one you had pictured in your mind. The director, most likely, is as excited about the motion picture as you are, but his or her vision of it may not correspond to yours.

By now you are positive that you, and only you, ought to direct your picture. You are the only person able to bring your mind's image to the screen.

Hold your horses.

Unless you are a *skilled* director, chances are that your film, regardless of the validity of your vision, will end up a failure—an amateur's attempt at best, not the viable expression of cinematic art it deserves to be. Don't forget, you are *not* a director as yet, but an expert in any one of the other cinematic areas; therefore, you look at the motion picture to be directed from your point of view, not the director's.

You, the screenwriter, expect to see the scenes you have written on the screen.

You, the actor, intend to explore the characters' emotional life.

You, the cinematographer, are ready to create unforgettable visual moments.

You, the producer, are tired of handing your vision over to a "bunch of creative nuts" who see you merely as an accountant, not the artistic force you are.

But: It is the *director* who is fully aware that the writer, actor, and cinematographer are but parts of the cinematographic *expression* being forged from a multitude of elements. It is the director who is responsible for expressing the film's story, theme, and mood in a *visual way*.

Obviously you, the beginning director, must study this visual approach to your matrix. You must learn all about a new, exhilarating, and often frustrating craft. Whether you choose to attend a film school or prefer to learn by observation working for a production company, you must be familiar with the basics of directing a motion picture. You must know about the structure of a viable motion picture script, you must know about acting *and* actors, you must know about music and sound. Most important, you must know about camera angles, setups, and moves, as well as editing techniques. Only then will you be able to bring your vision, your message, and your personal style to the screen.

Yet gaining proficiency is not a matter of memorizing a list of basic rules, it is the ability to gain mastery of technical skills, for these are the channels of your creative power. Marcel Proust put it very clearly: "But in art excuses count for nothing—good intentions are of no avail." In other words, talent and creativity count little if not backed up by craft.

Unfortunately some beginning directors rely too heavily upon the myth that their personal style and expertise in one of the related cinematic fields will pull them through their first directing assignment. They are the ones who believe in other myths as well:

I do not have to know anything about camera setups, movements, or angles. I let the cinematographer worry about those.

Wrong. Deciding about camera work is one of the most exciting aspects of directing a motion picture. By all means consult with your cinematographer. Listen to his or her advice; the cinematographer is an expert and knows what to do. But the decision is up to *you*. You give your motion picture its look and feel; after all, camera work does play an important part in giving a film its specific mood.

I do not have to worry about any mistakes. It's the editor's job to correct them.

If you failed to *cover*, if you failed to *match*, and if you misdirected on-screen movements (screen directions)—in short, if you as director have not done your homework—there is little an editor, even the best one, can do.

I will save time and money by using three cameras simultaneously.

Agreed, multimillion-dollar productions, even television films, employ the three-camera system. But you should not follow suit unless you own and operate a money-printing machine.

I do not have to shoot a full-length film. I'll produce a trailer and will interest an established production company in a coproduction.

Directors who believe in this myth will make the most costly mistake in their careers. Again and again during my lectures I have to look at happy faces and listen to excited voices telling me: "I've just completed my trailer—well, it cost about twenty thousand dollars—and now I'll show it around to investors and production companies." The sad fact is, though these beginning directors have sunk all their assets into the project or gone into debt, all this money is lost. No reliable production company will join forces with a neophyte, no investor will risk one penny on an unfinished motion picture regardless of how impressive the trailer is, if a novice director helms the project.

On the other hand, you'll have some chance of finding a distributor who will come up with the postproduction money if your motion picture is at least available in a raw cut.

I'll take my film (or script) to one of the film markets—Cannes, France; Milan (MIFED), Italy; Los Angeles—where I will meet people and interest them in my project.

Save your money. No one, except a few con artists out for a free drink, will even talk to you. You won't get admission to any of the exhibition halls. Admission (by ticket only) is reserved to exhibitors, distributors, and film buyers.

Take my advice, and don't ever rely on any of the above myths. They won't get you anywhere. Rely on your creative ability, and have the *craft* to back you up as you take step after step in pursuit of success. The motion picture industry does not abound with creative, talented, and *skilled* filmmakers. Eventually you will succeed.

But don't get discouraged if your progress seems slow. Don't we all know about the "overnight success" that took ten years to be achieved? Be ready for setbacks; accept failures as a learning experience; *and don't give up.*

Hang in there, and you'll make it as a filmmaker and director. So let's start working.

1.

The Director

and the

Screenplay

You have written or optioned a motion picture script. You are all fired up; you must see the exciting story on the screen. You can't wait to commence shooting. I know the feeling; I have been through it many times.

But now is the time to wait. Stand back. Gain some distance from the images churning in your mind. Wait until you are able to look at your script with—hopefully—unbiased "director's eyes." Remember, audiences do not attend motion pictures because of the actor's sensitive interpretations, the cinematographer's admirable work, or the director's skill. No, audiences attend motion pictures because they want to see a *gripping story*—a story that you, the director (unbeknownst to them), have brought in *on time* and *on budget*.

Since this book is about directing a motion picture, it covers only the essentials a beginning director ought to know about script structure. There are a number of excellent books on script writing on the market, and you should familiarize yourself with some of them.

In this chapter we will discuss the following:

Basic budgetary considerations
Script construction

Dialog
Screenplay development
    Rewriting original script in *visual* language
    Rewriting scenes into a shooting script (combined
        shot list/camera setup list)

Basic Budgetary Considerations

First you'll have to decide whether or not your script may be too demanding for the beginning director's admittedly meager budget.

Does the story require car chases, helicopter shots, or any other extensive action scenes?

Stunts are time consuming and will add shooting days to your budget. You ought to consider the cost of stunt vehicles and stuntmen, and last but not least the fact that your liability insurance will skyrocket the moment stunts have been added to the script.

Are the required special effects too ambitious for your budget?

If done ingeniously, special effects do not have to cost an arm and a leg. (Some advice on this will come in chapter 9.)

Is the script too verbal?

Remember, unlike a stage play, a motion picture is a visual medium. Therefore ask yourself, "Where should I substitute or strengthen verbal expression by the use of visual expression?"

Do you really need a cast of thousands?

Most likely you will be able to omit or consolidate some of the characters in the script.

Are too many different and/or expensive locations required?

If possible, forgo any location that demands an extensive travel budget. Try to find an equally satisfactory location close to home. If the expensive location will add to the film's production values, by all means splurge on it, but find ways to limit your use of the location. (More advice about this may be found in chapter 2.)

Script Construction

Each screenplay (script) has a beginning, a middle, and an end, or—if you will—Act I, Act II, and Act III as customary in a stage play, only the action is not nearly as evenly distributed as in a stage play. The screenplay offers a short beginning (Act I), a lengthy middle (Act II), and a short ending (Act III). You, the beginning director, should consider limiting your screenplay to ninety minutes on-screen time. Each additional five or ten minutes will increase your budget, and often the added expenditure does not justify the end product. Considered this way, a script looks something like this:

20 pages beginning
65 middle
15 end

Your script should contain no fewer than 100 and no more than 110 pages to cover the 90 minutes on-screen time. The rule of thumb is, one page of script equals one minute on-screen time. It is important to remember that the same basic script structure, as discussed in the pages that follow, applies to all films, not to suspense-type motion pictures only.

After you have made your decision about the script's budgetary requirements and its viability, you should ask yourself some pertinent questions:

- Does the screenplay as written show and anticipate the story's mood and atmosphere?
- Have the Who and Where been established clearly?
- Does the script contain any twists, and are those placed correctly?
- Do What and Why grow out of the relationship between the main characters, or have they been imposed on this relationship for the purpose of creating an exciting plot?
- Has the main question been asked correctly, or does it give rise to a split goal?
- Is the subplot strong enough?
- Does Act II keep on developing, or does it lag?
- Have you built a strong ending, and answered the main question?

ESTABLISHING MOOD AND ATMOSPHERE

Unlike a television show, which zaps the viewer immediately into the story, the motion picture can afford a more leisurely approach. A TV show *must* grab the viewers' attention quickly, or they will switch channels. However, a viewer who has bought a movie ticket or has rented a videotape is more patient. (Of course, when your motion picture is being shown at the various film markets, you must interest prospective buyers within the first fifteen minutes. They will look at the first ten to fifteen minutes and the last ten minutes of a feature film. Still, you'll have plenty of time to establish mood and atmosphere.)

But we are getting ahead of ourselves. Let's go back to the beginning that sets the mood of your motion picture. For the purpose of illustration we'll use the script of my motion picture *Jungle Trap.** This is the background of the plot:

About fifty years ago a number of Peruvian investors turned a sacred Mali burial ground, located in the Amazon jungle, into a luxury hotel resort. Shortly after the hotel was completed, the Malis attacked. They killed the staff and guests and destroyed the hotel. They in turn were annihilated. The jungle claimed the hotel again. A group of anthropologists travels to the site to recover an ancient Mali ritual mask. Upon arrival, the anthropologists find the hotel in perfect condition, fully staffed but devoid of guests. The scientists stay in the hotel, unaware that they are living in a phantom place and being served by apparitions. The moment they realize the truth, they are trapped as ghostly Mali warriors attack them.

On the emotional level the plot deals with Chris, a photojournalist, who sees her marriage to Josh, the leader of the expedition, on the verge of destruction as he falls in love with his young and beautiful native assistant, Leila.

This is how the original script read:

Establishing Shot of City.

(Various angles. Cut to an imposing building. A car stops in front of it. CHRIS *gets out, walks toward the building, and enters. Establish sign: "Museum of Natural History.")*

---

*Jungle Trap, a Ciara Productions film, 1991.

Interior Museum. Hallway.
(Camera pans along the pristine, whitewashed walls that display a collection of South American Indian sculptures. CHRIS *approaches. Camera moves in and holds on* CHRIS *as she stops in front of a warrior's mask.)*

You can tell, this beginning did its very best *not* to establish any mood. Rewritten, however, it did give the audience an anticipatory sense of the spine-tingling mood that permeates this motion picture:

(Dark screen. The swishing, rumbling sound of an approaching storm sweeps over us as slowly, ever so slowly, a number of indistinguishable shapes emerge from the darkness. The storm grows more violent. Faces, machetes, masks, and fists flash—intercutting and superimposing one another—in quick succession across the screen. The shapes become more and more distinct, until ultimately the Shock Zoom of a shrunken head, grinning, attacks the viewer. A high, piercing sound drowns out the storm.

Then, all of a sudden, silence takes over. Camera pulls back, revealing the shrunken head neatly displayed in a glass case. Camera pulls back farther to take in CHRIS. *She stops for a beat in front of the glass case, shakes her head. Camera pans with her as she continues down the hallway to a door marked "Director of South American Displays.")*

Now the beginning, obviously, is more in the line with the needed sense of eerie anticipation.

ESTABLISHING WHO AND WHERE

Some scripts make the mistake of revealing the What (what is going to happen) and Why (the motive for the main character's actions) just a little too early. Yes, the audience must know about the What and Why, but first it has to meet the main characters (Who) before it will care about what is happening to them. *Jungle Trap* features three main characters:

Chris, a photojournalist and anthropologist
Josh, her husband, an anthropologist
Leila, Josh's young assistant

The relationship between the main characters (Who) and their environment (Where) should be made known as early as possible. It is this relationship that explains the Why.

PLACING TWISTS

If the script contains any twists, they must be placed correctly.

• *Twist at the end of Act I:* An event occurs that sets up the main plot (What) and the main characters' motives subplot (Why). These motives lead the protagonist's (hero's) goal and the antagonist's (villain's) countergoal. This twist asks the main question: "Will _____ achieve this or that?"

• *Twist 1 in the middle of Act II:* Keeps the story going, possibly turns it in a different direction, and repeats the main question.

• *Twist 2 at the end of Act II:* Pulls the story toward Act III and to the plot's climax and denouement.

ESTABLISHING THE MAIN PLOT

The What and Why of the story must grow out of the relationship between the main characters, not just be imposed on it for the purpose of creating an exciting plot. In *Jungle Trap* Josh is very much taken with his young and beautiful assistant. Chris fears for her marriage. Leila is after Chris's husband *and* her job at the museum. The What and Why set the story in motion:

What the story is about determines the main plot and the film's line of action. *Why* determines the main characters' motives, leading to goal and countergoal. *Why* establishes the film's subplot and examines its theme.

The What in *Jungle Trap* sets the main plot in action: the anthropologists commence their expedition in search of the sacred Mali warrior mask.

As we look at the Why, we discover that Chris and Leila are the pivotal characters. It is their Why that supplies them with goals:

Chris's goal: I want to save my marriage by showing Josh that I'm a better woman and better scientist than Leila is.

Leila (countergoal): I want to destroy Chris's marriage by destroying her reputation as a scientist.

FRAMING THE MAIN QUESTION

If the main question has not been asked correctly, it will give rise to a split goal. Chris's character, in contrast to the aggressive Leila, has been established as pliable and soft. Her goal, as mentioned earlier, is:

> I want to save my marriage by showing Josh that I am
> a better woman and better scientist than Leila is.

If Chris's goal were to be stated this way:

> I want to save my marriage.
> I want to get hold of the ceremonial mask.

then we would be faced with a split goal. A split goal pulls a story in two different directions. The above split goal would result in the main question: "Will Chris save her marriage?" This main question, however, would end the film at the end of Act II, when Josh asks Chris for a divorce.

STRENGTHENING THE SUBPLOT

The subplot reveals the human element of your story. It gives your story depth and keeps your characters from becoming cardboard figures; it demands the audience's empathy. Here are some guidelines:

• The subplot must be part of the story, not a story by itself. While the main plot tells the story, the subplot focuses on the relationship between people. Often the subplot is the stronger and more interesting one, but it is the plot that causes the actions the characters take, and as such it holds the film together. (For example, in *Kramer vs. Kramer* the subplot deals with the couple's relationship to each other; the plot deals with the custody case.)

• Once you have clarified your plot-subplot structure you will have to check the structure of the subplot. The subplot has the same structure as the main plot, with a beginning, a middle, and an end. It also has twists of its own.

• The subplot twists should be placed as closely as possible to their respective main plot twists. If you are struggling with a script, most likely you are facing faulty main plot–subplot integrations.

BUILDING THE MIDDLE

(Act II)

Act II is the area where your screenplay should develop into an increasingly gripping matrix. At times, unfortunately, Act II may drag after an interesting beginning (Act I). Besides main plot and subplot twists and the integration of both, you need the following to keep Act II alive and kicking:

• Momentum (graduation, suspense)
• Foreshadowing
• Dark moment
• Highlight scenes
• Obstacles and conflicts

Momentum   Momentum simply means that a story gains in strength. This is achieved by the application of *graduation* and *suspense*.

Graduation   Check your story: Are *all* events on the same high or low interest level, or do they vary in strength? The interest level must move up, even though you should give your audience plateaus when "nothing much happens." The final (and highest) graduation should lead into the Dark Moment and from there into the last twist that propels the story into Act III. In *Jungle Trap* the final graduation begins when the Mali ghost warriors attack the hotel, and ends in the twist when Chris and Leila, the only survivors, have to join forces to escape being killed.

Suspense   While graduation keeps the audience's interest alive, it is overlapping suspense that holds Act II together. Act II consists of a series of overlapping suspense sequences, each headed by a goal that has to be either frustrated or satisfied. The point is that a new overlapping suspense sequence begins before the denouement of the previous one. For instance:

- Suspense sequence A: Chris suspects the hotel is a phantom place.
- Goal: I want to find out whether my suspicion is correct.
- Suspense sequence B: The anthropologists fear an attack by the ghost warriors.
- Goal: We will have to protect ourselves.

Make certain that suspense sequence B has been set in motion before the denouement of suspense sequence A has been delivered.

The denouement of the various suspense sequences *must* be delivered at the end of Act II. Then only the main question remains to be answered.

Never fail to make your characters' expectations of the outcome clear to your audience. Remember, your audience *expects* some outcome. It is fun (and makes for an exciting film) to manipulate this expectation:

- The denouement does not happen as anticipated: surprise.
- The audience—at this point—does not expect a denouement: shock.
  (This technique was used to great effect in the original *Halloween*.)
- The denouement happens as expected: satisfaction.

It is obvious that an always satisfied anticipation becomes as boring as a continually frustrated expectation becomes annoying.

Foreshadowing Foreshadowing is another integral part of momentum. Any event needs to be foreshadowed twice. Audiences should not become aware of foreshadowing. They should remember, however, after the foreshadowed event has taken place.

Dark Moment The twist at the end of Act II features the Dark Moment, when everything seems lost. It is imperative that at this point the main plot twist and the subplot twist are closely integrated, and that the main plot twist moves the story in a different direction. The Dark Moment in *Jungle Trap* occurs when everyone but Chris and Leila has been killed.

Highlight Scene A highlight scene resembles a plot within a plot. The highlight scene is an excellent device to keep the middle of a motion picture from dragging. It is most effective if it occurs immediately after Twist 1.

- The highlight scene ought to be an integral part of your film; it should not take off on a tangent of its own.
- The highlight scene should not last more than five to seven minutes.
- A highlight scene, starting from a point of departure, features a beginning (Act I), a middle (Act II), and an end (Act III). A twist occurs at the end of Act II.

In *Jungle Trap* I used the following highlight scene:

- *Point of Departure:* Chris is convinced that she and the anthropologists are trapped in a phantom place.
- *Beginning:* After Josh and Leila laugh about her "insane" phobia, Chris tries to get help. By radio she tries to make contact with the outside world.
- *Twist:* Chris reaches a ham operator, who shrugs her SOS off as a bad joke.
- *Middle:* Chris, assisted by a number of supernatural incidents, convinces the anthropologists about the impending danger.
- *Twist:* Ready to defend themselves, the anthropologists barricade the lobby's entrance and windows.
- *Dark Moment:* In front of their eyes the hotel begins to crumble. Jungle overgrows the lobby, and there is no place for them to hide.
- *End:* The anthropologists expect the warriors to attack. The attack does not happen (audience expectation has been frustrated — surprise and heightened suspense), and the anthropologists live through a night of waiting and fear.

The highlight scene has a subplot: finally Chris and Josh find the courage to discuss their marriage honestly.

Obstacles/Conflicts   Obstacles are barriers that keep a character from reaching his or her goal. Obstacles are important as they give you, the beginning director, the chance to "prove character in action" — that is, a character has to react to obstacles in keeping with *his or her established personality*. A braggart will not react humbly. A sensible person will not turn reckless, unless the secondary trait of recklessness has been established (foreshadowed) prior to the event.

Obstacles are closely connected to conflicts. All conflicts need to be established clearly, and at times they may need to be foreshadowed. Never expect your audience to guess at who is in conflict with whom or what, *but spell it out.* Only three conflict patterns are possible:

Man against man
Man against nature
Man against himself

If your script lacks suspense, I recommend that you investigate the obstacle/conflict area. Ask yourself:

Has obstacle or conflict been established early enough to cause audience anticipation?

Do the opposing forces have an equal chance to reach their goal? If not, your script will lack suspense. If John and Jerry court Miss Beautiful, but all advantages are on John's side, no suspense is evoked. But if the chance of success is equally distributed between the two, then we, the audience, are interested in the outcome of the competition.

Are goal and countergoal clearly stated, and are both focused upon the same area? Mary and Beth are both up for the starring role in an off-Broadway play. The girls are equally compelled to win the role, but they have never met, and do not know of each other's existence: same goal, but no conflict, and therefore no suspense. But if Mary and Beth are friends, and devious Beth does everything in her power to discredit sweet Mary, then we have a countergoal, with conflict and suspense.

CREATING THE STRONGEST END

(Act III)

The twist of Act II leads *immediately* into Act III. I recommend that this twist be the strongest of the entire script. Once Act III has started,

- Do not introduce any new characters
- Do not introduce any new events
- End your subplot before the climax of Act III begins.

Let the climax unfold quickly. Do not extend it by another conversation, by another action scene or horror effect. Make certain that the main question has been answered and that all loose ends have been tied up.

A word of warning to you the writer-director: as you set out to write your screenplay, don't concern yourself about script structure — except beginning, middle, and end. Let your excitement pull you ahead. Have fun; forget about twists, as well as dialog and highlight scenes, for the moment. It is especially futile to worry about main plot and subplot integration until the first draft of your screenplay has been written. However, by the time you are ready to tackle the shooting script, it is imperative that all humps have been straightened out. A vague or faulty structure will cause editing problems and delays, as you and your editor frantically try to give your film plot logic and a clear sense of relationship.

DIAGRAM OF SCRIPT STRUCTURE

Act I

- Visualize the mood of your film in the very beginning.
- Establish the Where (place and time).
- Establish the Who (main characters).
- A plot twist changes the existing conditions and sets the story in motion. It establishes:
    - a. The main plot (the film's line of action)
    - b. The subplot (the film's theme)
        1. Main goal: Protagonist's goal
                    Antagonist's countergoal
        2. Subgoal: Protagonist's and antagonist's subgoals (or secondary character's main goals) lead to conflict.
- The twist in Act I poses the main question: "Will _____ achieve _____ ?"
    The main question cannot be answered until the denouement of Act III.

Act II

- Act II begins immediately after the twist of Act I and its ramifications have been established.
- Now is the time to check for:
    - a. Momentum (graduation and overlapping suspense sequences)
    - b. Obstacles and conflicts

- About the middle of Act II, the main plot twist (Twist #1) occurs. This twist coincides with subplot twist #1 of Act II. The subplot twist should be set shortly before or after the main plot twist.
- It is effective to set a highlight scene in close proximity to main plot twist #1 and subplot twist #1. The highlight scene keeps a script from dragging. It has the same basic structure as the script:
  a. Beginning, middle, and end
  b. A clearly established *point of departure*
  c. Twists that lead from one act to the next
  d. A dark moment
- Main plot twist #2 and subplot twist #2 propel the story into Act III. These twists are the strongest ones in the film.

Act III

- Do not:
  a. introduce any new characters
  b. introduce any new events
- End your subplot before the climax begins. The climax focuses on the main plot only.
- Let the climax build up swiftly.
- Tie up all loose ends.
- Answer the main question.

Dialog

Now your script is finished. But you are not yet ready to commence shooting; your homework has not been finished. All dialog demands close scrutiny.

- Keep all speeches *short*. If some of the speeches are too long, divide them between two or more characters.
- Characters should *not* sound alike.
- Keep your dialog lean; trim off any unnecessary description, stilted words, or elegant turns of speech. Develop an ear for the everyday speech the average person uses.
- Have the dialog consistent with the area and/or time your film takes place. A Massachusetts fisherman speaks differently from a New York taxi driver or a Hollywood parking valet.

- Dialog should reflect the character's emotional state.
- Dialog—at times—should reveal conflict.
- Be aware that motion pictures are a *visual* art form; what your character says is not as important as what your character thinks or feels. Choose camera-trained actors who are able to express thoughts and emotions in a subtle way.
- Let your dialog reveal emotion. Permit differences in the way your characters:
  1. Comprehend and look at things
  2. Think and feel
  Don't ever forget about a dialog's emotional content.

Dialog is not easy to write. I cannot stress enough that it should *speak well*. Quite often, lines that read well may sound stilted and too polished once actors speak them. Ask your writer to rewrite dialog. The rewrite should take place during preproduction. Please do not surprise your actors with rewritten pages the moment they enter their dressing rooms.

Once dialog resembles everyday speech, it should reveal:

Character
Emotional state of mind
Emotional relationship
Conflict (if appropriate)

TRAITS AND MANNERISMS

(Characterization)

Most scriptwriters stress a character's traits and mannerisms. Some writers are very specific in the way they describe their characters. William may see an old man like this: "Jonathan stands like a tree that refuses to be felled. His eyes, in a face beaten by years in sun, wind, and biting snow, search the horizon with still-youthful vigor. Only his hands, now gnarled from hard work, reveal the ebbing strength of his body." And Elinor may state: "The old man, Jonathan, tries to keep going, but his body is ready to give up."

Regardless how much—or little—characterization a writer bestows upon his script, my advice is, forget about characterization for now. Go back to characterization once you are ready to cast the film. At this point go easy on what the writer has written about looks, traits, and mannerisms, and leave yourself open to whatever the actors' interpretation may be. Writers notoriously are not the best actors, and their character descriptions might lead you down the primrose path of cliché. But once you are involved in the casting process, *do* take traits and mannerisms seriously. After all, believable and creative characterization helps to shape the visual impact of your motion picture.

Traditionally, characterization provides the audience with clues to:

Physical traits/mannerisms
Personal traits/mannerisms
Emotional traits

Well, let this be all for now. In chapter 5, "The Director and Actors," we will tackle the problems of characterization.

Screenplay Development

The director's real homework starts once the script has been structured, and possibly rewritten, to your satisfaction. You will work on:

- Shooting script
- Once locations have been set:
    1. Continuity (in cooperation with the script supervisor*)
    2. Shooting and camera setup list.

And always keep in mind: you, the director, are responsible for the artistic and budgetary viability of your motion picture.

The following is a scene from *Jungle Trap*. It shows the script as written by the screenwriters.

---

*The script supervisor is responsible for taking notes throughout the production. These notes include directional notes such as "camera left, look" or "carried purse on right arm." Directional notes are important for the matching of shots in various angles (one shot flowing logically and smoothly into another).

Interior Hotel. Hallway. Night.
(On CHRIS *and* OBY, *the bellhop, approaching.* OBY *carries* CHRIS's *duffel bag. He opens a door and motions* CHRIS *to enter.)*
Interior Hotel. Chris's Room. Night.
*(*CHRIS *enters, followed by* OBY. OBY *places the duffel bag on her bed.* CHRIS *stands motionless as her eyes travel from corner to corner of the room.)*

OBY: I hope the room meets with your approval, madame.

CHRIS: Yes, it does. Thank you.

(She takes off her shoulder bag. She opens it. But suddenly her attention is caught by some perfume bottles and makeup items on the dressing table.)

CHRIS: But someone . . . apparently . . . lives here.

*(*OBY *smiles. It is a plastic, half-mocking, half-threatening smile.)*

OBY: Living is a metaphor . . . the idea is an abstraction.

CHRIS: Remove these things, please.

*(*OBY *walks over to the dressing table. He collects perfume bottles, powder box, and lipsticks. Again he smiles.)*

OBY: Living is . . . relative.

(By now CHRIS, *searching through her shoulder bag, has found a dollar bill. Ready to hand it to* OBY, *she turns. But* OBY *has disappeared. In his place a rocking chair rocks back and forth gently.* CHRIS *closes her eyes. As she opens them, the rocking chair has disappeared.* OBY, *hand outstretched, smiles at her.* CHRIS *hands him the dollar bill.)*

CHRIS: I seem to be seeing things . . . I'm exhausted.

OBY: Your journey was long and arduous.

(He pockets the money.)

OBY: Merci, madame.

*(*OBY *leaves. At the door he turns.)*

OBY: Dinner will be served at eight o'clock.

CHRIS: Thank you.

(Tired to her bones, she sits on the bed. She opens the duffel bag, and as she does, her gaze travels to the dressing table. Sparkling and glistening tauntingly, the perfume bottles and makeup items are back on the dressing table. CHRIS closes her eyes. As she opens them, she sees the makeup items are gone.)

CHRIS: I'm seeing things . . . Well, I better start unpacking. Hope they don't expect me to dress for dinner.

(She pulls some slacks and shirts out of her duffel bag. All of a sudden there is a puzzled expression on her face. She digs deeper into the bag, gets hold of something, pulls it out. A shrunken head grins at her. CHRIS stifles a scream as laughter echoes softly through the room.)

The following is the same scene after the director—at times helped by the screenwriter—has written the visual translation of the original script.

Interior Hotel. Hallway. Night.
300* *(On CHRIS and OBY, the bellhop, approaching. OBY carries CHRIS's duffel bag. He opens one of the doors and motions CHRIS to enter.)*
Interior Hotel. Chris's Room. Night.
(Note—Light plot: soft, almost diffused basic lighting, contrasted by slashing shadows and bright highlights on the dressing table.
301 *(CHRIS enters. OBY follows her. Pan with him as he walks to the bed and places CHRIS's duffel bag on it. Smiling a plastic, half-mocking, half-threatening smile, he turns to CHRIS.*
302 *Pull in on CHRIS. Medium Shot. She looks around.*
303 *CHRIS's point of view [POV]. The bed, shadows slashing across it. Hand-held camera to dressing table and the mirror. OBY's reflection hovers like an evil shadow.*
304 *Back on CHRIS. A slight shiver runs through her body. She crosses her arms protectively. But then, lifting her chin, she forces herself to calm down. Immediately something else catches her attention.*
305 *CHRIS's POV. The open window, curtains moving slightly in the night breeze [hand-held camera].*
306 *Back on CHRIS, Medium Shot, then Pull Back.)*

---

*Three-digit numerals preceding directions refer to camera setups.

Voice-over (VO) OBY: I hope the room meets with your approval . . .

(OBY steps into frame.)

OBY: . . . madame.

*(CHRIS's eyes are still focused in the direction of the window.
[NOTE—Watch eye level and direction])*

CHRIS: Yes, it does . . .

(She turns to OBY.)

CHRIS: . . . thank you.

(Searching for a tip, CHRIS opens her shoulder bag, but—again—she becomes distracted.)
307 *(CHRIS's POV. Hand-held camera on dressing table. Bright highlights glitter on perfume bottles, on a powder box, and on two or three opened lipsticks.*
308 *Back on CHRIS and OBY.)*

CHRIS: But someone . . . apparently . . . lives here.

OBY *(smiles):* Living is a metaphor . . . the idea is an abstraction.

CHRIS: Remove these things, please.

309 *(Pan with OBY as he walks to the dressing table. OBY collects the makeup.)*
OBY: Living is . . .

(Pan with OBY as he walks back to where CHRIS stands.)

OBY: . . . relative.

(By now CHRIS has found a dollar bill. She turns to OBY.
310 *Tight Medium on CHRIS, startled.*
311 *CHRIS's POV. OBY has disappeared. In his place a rocking chair rocks back and forth gently. We hear a slight creaking sound. Flash cuts: hand-held camera [NOTE—For editing: flash cuts increase in speed]*
312 *On CHRIS*
313 *On rocking chair*

314 *On* CHRIS

315 *On* OBY, *extreme closeup [CU]. He smiles.*

315A *Low angle on* OBY

315B *High angle on* OBY

315C *Zoom Shot on* OBY, *and hold on* OBY. *His voice seems to come from far away.)*

OBY: Your journey was long and arduous.

316 *(Back on* OBY *and* CHRIS. *She hands him a dollar bill.* OBY *pockets the money.)*

OBY: Merci, madame. Dinner will be served at eight o'clock.

*(*OBY *walks out of frame. Pull Out as* CHRIS *walks toward the bed. Suddenly she stops, her body tenses.*

317 CHRIS's *POV. The dressing table. The makeup items are back [hand-held camera]. The perfume bottles glitter harshly.*

318 *Back on* CHRIS. *First puzzled, then frightened.*

319 *Back on the dressing table. It is empty [hand-held camera].*

320 *Pan with* CHRIS *as she walks to the bed, flops down on it. For a beat she sits motionless, hands folded in her lap, head down, her back rounded. Then she stretches, and—every movement showing how tired she is—she opens her duffel bag. She yawns, curls up next to her duffel bag.)*

CHRIS: Hope they don't expect me to get dressed for dinner.

(Grinning to herself, she stretches again and finally begins to pull some clothes—slacks and shirts—out of the bag. She digs deeper into her bag.)

CHRIS: Where is my . . .

(She continues searching for something.)

CHRIS: . . . must have forgotten it. So what . . .

(She digs deeper into her duffel bag. Stops. She reaches for something, and—a puzzled expression on her face—begins to explore it.

321 *CU on* CHRIS's *hand holding an item.*

322 *Tight Medium as* CHRIS *pulls something out of her duffel bag.*

323 *Shock Zoom on a shrunken head, grinning in* CHRIS's *hand.*
324 *Medium Shot on* CHRIS. *Still holding the shrunken head, she stifles a scream. Soft laughter echoes through the room.)*

As you compare the visual script with the original script you will notice:

• On the page the visual script appears longer than the original script. Don't worry that your film may run over the cost-effective ninety minutes' length. On-screen minutes are based upon the original script, not the visual script.

• The dialog was not changed. It was lean and precise to begin with, but has been *integrated* with camera and actors' movements. Chris's lines about "seeing things" have been omitted and replaced with visual elements.

• All visual elements were expanded upon.

• Camera movements and setups plus the appropriate numbers have been decided upon and written in. Many directors do not add numbers and camera setups at this time, but work on the script's visual elements only. They prefer to write a more extensive shot list (shooting script).

This particular scene does not require intricate camera moves. I felt the otherworldliness had to be created by Oby's smile and a lighting plot that contrasted soft basic lighting with harsh shadows and burning highlights. Since this scene did require a lengthy light setup, I saved time by going easy on camera moves and setup, and by using a hand-held camera whenever possible.

Shooting Script

(Combined Shot List/Camera Setup List)

Do not write your shot list until you have your locations contracted. Once you have your locations, you may be forced to adjust or simplify some elements of your shooting script. Now is the time to work closely together with your cinematographer, as you pay close attention to the *time element* involved in shooting each scene:

- How much time is required to set up the basic light plot for a location?
- How much time is required to adjust lights for each camera setup?
- How much time is required to shoot each segment of every scene?
- Have you allowed plenty of rehearsal time for intricate actor-camera moves?

For you, the beginning director who will, most likely, begin your career directing a low (very low)-budget film, it is imperative that you set a brisk—but achievable—time schedule for each shooting day.

I recommend that you neither stress out your actors and crew by breathing down their necks, nor lose authority by permitting too leisurely setups. For a nonunion film the following time schedule should work well:

7–9 A.M.	Setup time.	Lighting crew, prop and set crew setup. Makeup for actors. AD works with actors on lines. Director and cinematographer discuss day's work. Consult with script supervisor.
9 A.M.–2 P.M.	Shoot	
2–3 P.M.	Lunch break	
3–8 P.M.	Shoot	

Such a strenuous shooting schedule applies to the nonunion, weekend shoot *only*. If you are to shoot five days in a row you'll have to readjust your schedule to a somewhat easier pace. A union film (SAG [Screen Actors Guild] actors but nonunion crew) has schedule requirements (meal penalty, overtime, TDY*) that change somewhat from area to area. In case you are shooting a SAG film, have your production manager check out individual requirements.

*TDY stands for "temporary duty," a military expression that has become popular in the film industry. It is used to describe travel, lodging, and meal expenses en route to locations and sometimes on location as well.

SHOT LIST

The following shot list (shooting script) shows the various camera setups and camera moves needed in the scene. In this scene we have four camera setups. Setup I is at the door, setup II is at the dressing table, setup III refers to the hand-held camera sequence, and setup IV takes place at the bed. As you will notice, the camera setup numbers are not in consecutive order; they do not follow the scene's logical flow, but take into consideration only where the action takes place. For example, camera setup I (at the door) begins with Oby's and Chris's entrance and ends with Oby's exit—that is to say, includes all action taking place at the door.

Camera Setup I   (one hour)

301 *(OBY and* CHRIS *enter room*
302 *Camera moves in on* CHRIS
304 *On* CHRIS
306 *On* CHRIS. *Camera Pull Back.*
308
310
312
314
318
316
308 *On* CHRIS *and* OBY—*Pan as* OBY *walks to door.)*

Camera Setup II   (dressing table)   (one hour)
303
317
315
309 *(Pan with* OBY *as he goes to dressing table.*
311 *On rocking chair*
313 *On rocking chair)*

Camera Setup III   (hand-held on OBY)   (a few minutes)
315, 315A, 315B, 315C

Camera Setup IV   (bed)   (one hour)

316 *(Pan with* CHRIS *as she walks to the bed.*

320

322

324

321 *CU on item in duffel bag.*

323 *Zoom Shot on shrunken head.)*

The Director

and the

Budget

Motion picture budgets have skyrocketed during the past few years. A budget of $40 million for a production mounted by a major studio sounds quite reasonable these days. Before we discuss your budgetary responsibility as a beginning director, it might be beneficial to scrutinize your film's distribution possibilities.

Distribution of Small Films

It is more than unlikely that you will be entrusted with a budget that carries a $5 million tag. Your film, if you are fortunate, will have to be produced on a budget of, say, $250,000 to $500,000. While such an amount sounds adequate for a small film, it is, in actuality, hardly sufficient to produce a film sellable in today's market. There are many small, artistically and technically excellent films around, as well as a host of mediocre action and horror films. These are the projects that will give you your first chance to direct. While a few of these films will enjoy a short theatrical distribution in the United States, the majority will never do so.

Escalating advertising and promotional costs are the reason behind the theatrical nonexistence of small films. Typically one third of the cost of a film has to be earmarked for promotion. About $10 million for a major studio production, and from $500,000 to $2 million for the average small, independently distributed film, are considered to be reasonable advertising (PR) budgets.

But don't despair, don't give up your dreams of producing and directing your film. A small but healthy overseas market exists for your product. Admittedly, Japan, France, England, Canada, and Germany are not very receptive to small independents. But other European territories as well as Africa and the Far East provide a number of enthusiastic buyers, who look for the Hollywood label (United States–produced films) but are unable to spend a great deal of money. (The producer doesn't have to worry about language barriers. The respective buyers will dub the film, but the producer has to supply the buyers with sufficient numbers of black-and-white "stills" for lobby display and promotion.) Films are bought for theatrical as well as TV release, and for the lucrative video rental market. During the past few years Africa and the Far East have seen an explosion in the latter market and are looking for action, adventure, and horror films.

If a low-budget film is fortunate enough to find a small domestic theatrical* distribution company that will book it on a limited run (a week here, another week there), this film will make more money in the foreign market than would the U.S. theatrical undistributed film, and it has a good chance to be picked up by one of the bigger domestic video rental distributors. At times small independent distributors, counting on the lucrative video rental release, are ready to lose money on the limited theatrical run of a picture. Without domestic theatrical release a small, low-budget film has little chance to interest a big video rental distributor. It may, however, be lucky enough to be accepted by one of the small ones.

The point I wish to make is this: do not set your hopes on your film's breaking box office records. (Yes, I have heard about "sleepers"—they are rare, very rare exceptions.) Don't expect your film to become a success, even a mild one, but be happy and satisfied if it finds some overseas distribution and a small niche among the domestic video rental releases. If you think about the many pictures remaining on the shelf, you may consider yourself fortunate to have your film out, have it compete with others, and have it

---

*"Theatrical" refers to exhibition in motion picture theaters.

make your name known a little. Who knows—somewhere down the line you may be directing a major picture for Columbia, Universal, Warner Brothers, or Paramount.

Budgets for Small Films

And now to the other side of the coin. A budget of even $250,000 may be out of line for you. You have no way of ever raising such an amount.

Don't give up.

A budget of this size refers to a film shot on 35mm raw stock, or as it is commonly called in the industry, a "35 film," but a sellable film shot on tape can be made for a fraction of that amount. To be honest, a taped film will be made for *home video use* only. And again, to be honest, the video rental distributors are still shying away from taped features. Still, if your film is artistically and technically sound, you will be able to interest some foreign video rental buyers and one or another of the small domestic home video distribution companies. (We will learn more about taped feature films later in this chapter.)

Remember, it is important to get your film *out in the market.* Don't sit at home thinking, "I hope I get a budget," or "I wish I knew some investors," or even worse, "One of these days . . ." *Get out and do your film!*

It is a sad truth that whenever a motion picture—regardless of the size of the budget—runs "over," the director has to take the blame for it. It doesn't matter that the film went over budget because the star—being late, requesting too many takes—held up the shooting schedule, or the producer had not done his or her homework, or unforeseen expenditures were unavoidable. The truth is, *all* accusing fingers will point at you, the director. It is, therefore, a good idea to become familiar with the budget items directly—at times indirectly—under your control:

Camera rental	Special effects
Raw stock	Actors
Editing	Stunts
Locations	

Discuss costs with the producer and agree on sums to be spent. Please don't join the ranks of those directors who firmly believe that the producer, being a money machine, has unlimited funds at his or her disposal.

CAMERA RENTAL

You'll save a great deal of money by utilizing weekend rates. Have your equipment (camera, lenses, magazines, tripod, sound and light equipment, etc.) picked up on Friday after 5 P.M., and return it before 10 A.M. Monday morning. If you are—and most likely you will be—on a tight budget, weekend rates are heaven sent. Ask your cinematographer to arrange for equipment rental, since he or she knows the rental places and is familiar with their equipment. Needless to say, all items must be returned *before* 10 A.M. Monday, or you'll have to pay for another day's rent. And don't forget to reserve your equipment about four weeks ahead of your first shooting day.

Make certain that the producer has arranged for equipment insurance. Any camera damage for which the production company has to pay will skyrocket your budget.

Do *not* permit a crew member to attempt any repair should equipment break down. The production company will be held responsible for damages resulting from the repair attempt. For this very reason it is imperative that you obtain the name and *home* telephone number of the rental house's owner or manager. In case of equipment breakdown, the rental house is responsible for the exchange, and the exchange has to take place *quickly.*

Make certain that the cinematographer has all the necessary items such as lenses, filters, magazines, etc. needed for the weekend shoot. You do not wish to waste shooting time while the production assistant rushes back to the rental house to pick up a forgotten item. At times, rather than wait, find alternative ways of shooting.

Before taking the camera out, have your cinematographer check it out thoroughly. Ignore any claims the rental house makes as to previous tests and equipment reliability.

- Check for camera scratches and light leaks by running a small amount of film through the camera and examining the *undeveloped* film for scratches.

- Focus a strong light on the *loaded* camera and develop the raw stock to show any light leaks in the equipment. This, of course, has to be done days ahead of your first shooting date.
- Check for blurred projection. In this case the camera shutter is out of synchronization.
- If the film goes in and out of focus, something is wrong with the camera's pressure plate.
- When using more than one camera check that individual frames and sprocket holes match. If they do not, the frame line will jump during the projection of the edited film.

Check microphones and recorders for any unusual noise. In editing most difficulties arise because of poor sound quality.

Reserve your expensive 35mm BL sync camera for dialog scenes only. Dialog scenes should take place on interior shots (indoors), where the sound environment can be controlled. If you must shoot a lengthy dialog exterior (outdoors), you will have to contend with unwanted sounds disturbing the scene. You should be able to correct some (not all) of them during the editing process by adding canned (recorded) sound that is in harmony with the environment. You may add traffic if the dialog takes place at a street corner, the roar of surf for your beach scene, and have birds chirping whenever you film a romantic garden scene. A more cost-efficient way, nevertheless, is the use of rear projection. (We will discuss rear projection a little later.)

If you are faced with a short dialog scene, you may decide to shoot MOS (without sound)* and dub the dialog in later; you do this by cutting "loops" of the actor's lines, which the actors must be able to lip-sync, and that are then edited in later. I would recommend this technique only if you have to loop a word here and there, since there is a noticeable difference between sync and looped sound.

For any scenes that require very little or no dialog, you will do well to use a nonsync camera. Such a camera is far less expensive than the BL sync camera, and you save setup time by eliminating the sound equipment.

---

*In the early thirties a German director used to say "motion, *mitout* sound," thus the term MOS.

THE THREE-CAMERA SYSTEM

If you are faced with tricky action shots (fights, car chases, car crashes, etc.), then—but only then—is the time ripe to rent three cameras. Forget about the fact that major productions use the three-camera system whenever the spirit moves them. Let me remind you, the three-camera system should be used for *action* scenes only; then, of course, three cameras are mandatory, since you may have only *one* chance to get a certain moment on film.

But let me explain why (besides the cost) the three-camera system won't work for you, the beginning director:

Three cameras are set up to shoot simultaneously a Full Shot, a Medium Shot, and a CU. Generally speaking, this does not work well, since actors move differently in each shot. The actor has sufficient space for movement in a Full Shot, less in a Medium Shot, and very little—if any—in a CU. Also, the actor's facial expression is far more subtle in the CU than in the Medium Shot.

The Full Shot, Medium Shot, and CU camera setups are effective for fight scenes. Most fight scenes are combinations of numerous *very short* takes, and you will use Neutral Shots (closeups of faces, fists, knives, etc.) to transit from one shot to the next.

For action scenes (car hits, car tumbling down a cliff, car exploding, etc.) you will set up your cameras at various angles. One camera shoots the action from front, the other two cameras shoot from the sides. Since none of these shots match in terms of direction (we will discuss camera movement and direction in Part II), this technique does represent an editorial problem, which you may overcome easily by adding Neutral Shots, such as CUs of faces, hands gripping a steering wheel, or a foot pumping brakes.

For three-camera shots you will rent an inexpensive non-sync 35mm combat camera.

RAW STOCK

Unexposed film is called raw stock. One minute of film takes ninety feet of 35mm raw stock and forty-five feet of 16mm raw stock. Add to that the ensuing lab costs (developing and 1 light work print, which is used to edit the rough cut), and raw stock constitutes a major expense.* Many beginning directors and producers are fond of shooting 16mm or even Super 8mm. I would like to discourage this practice. Of all the films I produced I shot only one in 16mm, and it was the one film that turned out to be a headache.

Granted, if you shoot 16mm you'll save on raw stock and lab cost. Granted, you can blow up a 16mm print into a 35mm print (not inexpensive), but there is always the chance that such an answer print will look grainy, and unless you have framed your 16mm meticulously, you'll be faced with very unattractive empty spots on either side of the frames, since a 35mm frame is *oblong* and a 16mm frame is *square*.

SHOOTING RATIOS

A shooting ratio of ten to one (on good days, five to one) is considered acceptable for the average low-budget film. You the beginning director with only a limited budget at your disposal would do well to limit yourself to a three-to-one shooting ratio—that is, you'll shoot *three* takes for every *one* take to be seen on-screen.

Theoretically you'll shoot 270 feet of 35mm raw stock for every minute seen on the screen. All of us, without any doubt, are aware that theory and practice are birds of different feathers. No producer will tie you, the director, to the stake of the three-to-one rule. Nevertheless, the three-to-one rule is a bitter reality; three to one is all you can *afford* to shoot. Decide, therefore, how much raw stock you can expend on each scene. Action scenes do require at least three (if not more) takes—one rule of thumb is to give each action scene about five takes—but dialog scenes should be brought in in two takes. This explains why you *must* employ skilled *motion picture* actors only. Forget about the brilliant actor you saw last month at a little theater performance; forget about your niece the aspiring actress who needs a break; forget about your writer who always dreamed about acting; and do hire skilled *motion picture actors* who:

Know how to hit a mark in front of a camera.

---

*The film you have shot will be developed in the lab, then stored in a vault. You will receive a work print, which the editor uses.

Know about moving and performing in front of a
    camera.
Know about the angles they have to use when in front
    of a camera.
Know how to express thought and emotions.

Any skilled motion picture actor will bring in a credible performance in the first take. But do take a second one for security. Having only one take is too risky.

EDITING

You'll save considerably on raw stock and lab costs if you "edit in the camera." But let me clear up a common misconception. Editing in the camera does not indicate that you will shoot scenes in the same sequence as they will appear on the screen. You are, after all, shooting a professional motion picture, and not a home movie. Editing in the camera means that you *won't* follow the traditional progression of shots:

Master Shot of entire scene (Full Shot) followed by:
Medium Shots (either Two-Shots or Reversal Shots of
    dialog and/or business) followed by:
Closeups of actors and/or objects

Once in a while the traditional way of shooting has its place, even for you the beginning director, but generally you'll edit in the camera by following your airtight shooting script that lists camera angles and movements. A tight shooting script is mandatory for the smooth flow of each day's shooting. It eliminates last-minute inspiration that may cause setup changes. Discuss the shooting script at length with your cinematographer, and pay close attention to such potential problem areas as "matching" and "directions" (both will be discussed in chapter 3).

Since we will discuss editing later, suffice it to say that you should work closely with the script supervisor, during preproduction and once the project is "on the floor." Meticulously kept records will save much editing waste later on.

LOCATIONS

If at all possible, avoid travel time and overnight stays. Both bear on a limited budget heavily. Do avoid travel from one location to the next during one day's shooting. For instance: You have planned a morning shoot in front of a small town's old-fashioned courthouse. Next on the agenda—right after lunch—is a beach location where your two young leads discuss Aunt Hilda's inheritance. It takes about two hours to travel from the courthouse to the beach. So why not scratch the beach location and substitute it with a location close by—say, one of the picturesque, tree-lined streets near the courthouse? Couldn't the dialog about Aunt Hilda take place just about anywhere?

Or: One of the scenes in your film takes place in the hallway of a college; the next scene—a short one—will be shot in an attorney's office. Why load up all your equipment? Why chase actors and crew from one place to the next? Why not "dress up" a college office appropriately?

Or: You have to shoot two living-room scenes. One takes place in the Browns' living room; the other takes place in the Smiths' living room. Both families are of equal socioeconomic background. Avoid going to two different locations for your interior shots. Have your art director set up both locations in the same house.

Avoid too many exterior locations. Agreed, you must have a number of exterior shots; they open your film and help set its mood. But exteriors are time consuming. If no action takes place, and if no particular atmosphere is needed, why not buy stock shots for your run-of-the-mill Establishing Shots of a place?

Avoid night shots. Night shots do require more equipment, including a generator, and are time consuming to set up. Still, night shots do add considerably to a film's mood, especially a suspense or horror film. Fortunately, the problem of expensive night shots can be overcome by shooting "day for night." All you need are special filters and plenty of sunshine, for it is the sunshine that translates to the most gorgeous moonlit night on the screen. Needless to say, if you want dark corners and threatening shadows to create a mood of apprehension, you have no other choice but to opt for a nighttime shoot. In case you need rain, you can rent a rain machine; if you hanker for fog, you can choose from a number of fog makers on the market.

By all means *do* utilize expensive locations, may these be a movie ranch for your action and car chase scenes, or the fabulous interior of an old mansion. Do not skimp on picturesque locations; they do add production value to your film, and they hide all the other corners you may have cut. Expensive locations can, and will, give your low-budget film the air of a major production. But: utilize your expensive location in a conservative way.

Shoot plenty of Establishing Shots, moving shots, as well as group scenes on the location, but choose a substitute location for all your lengthy dialog scenes. This is the way you do it:

Exterior, Expensive Location   Have your actors move into a Medium Shot against heavy foliage before their dialog commences.

Exterior, Inexpensive Location   Place your actors in front of heavy foliage (your backyard) in a Medium Shot, and shoot the dialog scene. Note that an exterior dialog scene should be shot only if there is little or no sound interference. You may opt for an interior shot instead and have your art director set up the foliage background in a studio. But let me warn you, there will *always* be a slight problem in lighting the scene. Outdoor light *is* different from indoor light. It may be more efficient to take a slide of the foliage background at the expensive location, go on an insert stage, and use the slide for rear projection, as such re-creating the original location. I have used this technique successfully several times. On the screen it was impossible to tell where the actual location ended and the substituted location (rear projection) began.

Interior, Expensive Location   Shoot all the establishing and moving shots you could possibly use (you need these for transitional shots between segments). Bring some of your own props, such as chairs, bric-a-brac, pictures, and move your actors in front of them. Finish the take in a Medium Shot.

Interior, Inexpensive Location   Have your art director paint a few flats to match the wall of the expensive location, place your props as these had been placed at the expensive location, move your actors in front of them, and shoot. Or take a slide of the expensive location and utilize the insert stage. Another word of warning: be aware that the small fan used to keep the slides cool *does* make a slight humming sound, so you will need some appropriate canned sounds to mask the hum.

MORE ADVICE

Discourage your cinematographer from installing scaffolding, wooden or steel beams attached to the ceiling to support lights. Admittedly, such lighting is extraordinary *if* you are on a sound stage that offers catwalks, but on location you should avoid this type of lighting. Setting up scaffolding is very time consuming, and the damage that scaffolding *will* do to walls and ceilings adds considerably to the producer's damage budget. Stand firm; scaffold lighting is *out.*

Building tracks is another time-consuming habit dearly beloved by some cinematographers. Commonly tracks are built to accommodate a camera that moves back or forth, while actors engaged in dialog walk in front of it. You, the beginning director, do not need tracks, but you *do* need a cinematographer who (with the help of a shoulder harness) is blessed with a steady hand. Seat him or her on a wheelchair pulled by a grip (you can rent a wheelchair at any place that rents medical supplies), and—presto—you do your tracking shots simply, easily, and cost effectively.

Always apply for location permits. In Los Angeles and New York (and any other large city) you will apply for permits at the appropriate city administrative office. The permits are very reasonable, but they do require that the production company shows *proof of insurance.* The producer (or production manager) has to list:

Number of cars to be parked
Number of people (cast and crew) on location
Use of generator, if applicable
Special effects, car chases, stunts, gunfights

In case you film car chases and/or gunfights, a fire marshal *must* be hired by the production company. If you have contracted for a location that has no fire hydrant close by, a fire truck and driver must be provided as well.

If you are filming at an exterior location way out in the sticks, please make certain that your production company provides a Port-a-Potty for cast and crew.

Check with your production manager to make *certain* that all location permits have been obtained. You do not want to arrive at your location, only to be sent home by the police. Incidentally, you need location permits for both exterior and interior locations.

Recently, at least here in Los Angeles, an interesting money-producing game has cropped up. Suddenly from the house to the right of your location, a boom box blasts, while in the backyard to your left someone keeps a chain saw in motion. If you want to shoot you'll have to pay for peace and quiet. But the moment you wave your location permit, the noisemakers are out of business.

SPECIAL EFFECTS

We will discuss this important area in chapter 9.

ACTORS

Since actors are the director's most important, pressing, and exciting responsibility, chapter 5, "The Director and Actors," has been devoted to them.

CREW

Here we are getting into a gray and often slippery area. Theoretically the crew is not the director's responsibility. It is the producer who, advised by the production manager and cinematographer, will hire the crew. Yet it is you, the director, who is responsible for their efficiency. Obviously, an inefficient crew will cause shooting delays. You should—gently—suggest to the producer that he or she:

- Hire only well-qualified personnel.
- Not rely completely on resumes, but talk to previous employers.
- Hire college students as assistants. Give them a chance to work and to learn.
- Stay away from smooth-talking drifters, who abound in this business.

STUNTS

The producer will hire the stunt coordinator, who, in turn, will hire the stuntmen. But it is you, the director, who together with the producer and stunt coordinator—are responsible for any mishap. Insist that the producer hire a well-qualified and experienced stunt coordinator. *Insist* (as will the insurance company) on sufficient insurance. *Insist* (as will the agency that is responsible for location permits) that a fire marshal, water truck, and driver be in attendance in case of car chases or car crashes. Though it is not mandatory, insist that a knowledgeable first-aid person be on the location whenever you film chases, fights, and shoot-outs.

The Taped Feature Film

And now to the taped feature film I mentioned previously. It is possible to bring in a taped feature film for about $30,000—a fraction of the cost of a 35mm or even 16mm film. But let me warn you, even if a taped film is technically and artistically as sound as any 35mm film, you will face difficulties in finding a well-established domestic video rental distributor, for the simple reason that your taped film had no theatrical distribution. But your film, no doubt, will find a comfortable niche in the smaller foreign video rental market, and it may even get a shot at the domestic market.

For you, the beginning director, it is imperative that you have a film out in the market. So why not tape your project?

We discussed financing at the beginning of this chapter, and as you will agree, it is unusual if not impossible for the beginning director-producer to secure financing—even a sum as small as $30,000—for a project. No one, not even kind Aunt Lucille, feels impelled to invest in your cinematographic future. But you believe in yourself, your friends believe in themselves. So get together a group of skilled and enthusiastic artists (a writer, a producer, a cinematographer, an art director, some lead actors) and finance your project the credit card way, as each of you contributes his or her services and a few thousand dollars.

A tape project will expose the involved artists' names and work to the market. A tape project, if artistically and technically sound, *will* find its market. Here are the advantages of a tape project over a film project:

• Three costly items are eliminated from the start. Using ¾" tape (and this *is* the format you will use) is not costly at all. Moreover, if a take doesn't meet your standards you'll erase it and start anew. Even better, you do not have to wait for "dailies" to see your mistakes. By viewing a scene immediately, you can make corrections on the spot.
You do not have lab expenses:
Developing and 1 light print
Negative cutting
Answer print
You do not have expensive sound-lab costs.

• Lighting is not as extensive and as complicated as it is in films. You will save on lighting equipment rentals and on crew.

• Opticals (not inexpensive on film) cost nothing if done during the taping, and titles (another costly item) cost next to nothing if done via character generator during the editing process.

• Some terrific special effects and even animation can be done on tape.

But don't even dream of saving money by enlisting your faithful camcorder. To have the technical edge over other projects, you must give the picture the *look* of a 35mm film by using the very best taping and editing equipment available. You may do well to earmark the main portion of your budget for equipment rentals and editing.

It is best to stay away from renting camera, sound equipment, and lights separately. Also, who knows whether your cinematographer is *really* familiar with the rented equipment? During the first few shooting days much time might be lost in learning about the camera.

I'd suggest that you hire a package that includes not only a cinematographer and assistant—who will be responsible for sound and lighting—but also camera, sound equipment, and lights. In Hollywood such a package can be rented for about $1,200 to $1,500 per day. (You do not pay for equipment insurance.) And, of course, since you will be shooting between ten and twelve days, you will negotiate for a discount.

Find out whether the cinematographer who owns the package is versed in taping commercials, industrials, and—hopefully—feature films. Stay away from one who specializes in weddings and family gatherings; such a person lacks the experience you need.

Editing a taped film, no question about that, is expensive. Editing time, including the operator, may range from $35 to about $115 per hour. (You will arrange for a discount.) Your taped film requires—after extensive pre-editing—about fifty to seventy editing hours.

You should supervise the editing process and do the pre-editing yourself. For this purpose have the ¾″ tape—adding time codes—transferred to a ½″ tape. Time codes, numbers that count minutes and (in rapid succession) seconds, are the key to pre-editing. Rent a VCR that comes equipped with a counting device, and going over and over your tapes, do your pre-editing at home.

This task, nerve-racking at first, will go smoothly as soon as you have become accustomed to the insane dance of numbers in front of your eyes. You will write down:

Reel #
Number count on VCR
Time code
Scene synopsis

PRE-EDITING LIST FOR TAPED FILM

Reel #	Number count on VCR	Time code	Synopsis
R 10	211	5:7–6:28	Est. high rise
R 3	85	32:53–33:06	Lil at bus stop
		Kitchen Scene	
R 3	155	2:35–4:22	"I have good news ..."
R 3	170	4:30–5:40	CU
R 3	186	55:06–56:02	Lil walks to corner Medium Shot

Why Low-Budget Motion Pictures Go Over Budget

Director Has Not Done His or Her Homework.

Director Has Not Done His or Her Homework.

Director Has Not . . . You get the idea!

Ego Clashes A great many films go over budget because ego clashes cause lengthy (and stubborn) arguments on the set. Ego problems may exist between:

> Director and writer
> Director and producer
> Director and cinematographer
> Director and actor
> Director and production manager
> Actor and actor

Leave your ego at home. Know when to compromise or even give in, and when to stand firm. Don't forget it is you, the director, who helms the project. To keep the shoot flowing smoothly, try to gauge personalities during the preproduction period. Keep an ear and eye open for any personality quirks that may cause difficulties later on.

The person you most likely may encounter difficulties with is the production manager. Undeniably it is his or her responsibility to keep the show rolling, to avoid delays, and to get all scheduled setups "into the can." This responsibility naturally offers built-in opportunities for clashes. First of all, let the production manager know that while you appreciate all this help, you are the one at the helm once the production is on the floor. Recognize that it is he or she who is in full command of crew, catering, transportation, location permits, location arrangements, procuring of raw stock, equipment rental, and liaison with lab and sound lab—in short, all elements that will help or hinder your responsibility of *directing* the film. Do not permit the production manager to infringe on your responsibility. Second, win his or her respect by having done your homework, and by bringing in the scheduled setups for each day. Third, make it clear that you are equally concerned about bringing the film in on time and on budget.

Rewrites on the Set   Among the most annoying and time-wasting devices are those last-minute "inspired" rewrites on the set. Actors bristle the moment they see changes. Don't blame them. They have created a character based on the original text. Any change may make their interpretation opaque.

Rewrites on the set are especially damaging to a suspense film, in which action and dialog are so closely hinged together that changes may obscure the plot.

All rewrites should be done during the preproduction period.

Actors   Actors unskilled in motion picture acting techniques can ruin a low-budget motion picture's shooting schedule.

Unskilled Key Personnel   If any of your key personnel should prove to be unskilled or overly argumentative, you have no choice but to replace this person with one better suited.

Too Many Takes On One Scene   Know when to splurge and know when to conserve expensive raw stock. Don't expect every scene to be perfect; minor flaws—if you have shot enough coverage—will be taken care of in editing. At times, clever use of coverage may save your day, by straightening out a potential problem, such as I experienced in making one of my films:

One of our actresses, a lovely girl, had been cast for her beauty, not for her skill in front of the camera. Repeatedly she blew her lines, moved out of frame, could not hit her mark. Raw stock was wasted; time was wasted. Before things could get any worse, we took some (silent) reaction shots of her, and—and since this particular scene took place in a small restaurant—we took the opportunity to shoot many reaction shots of the extras assembled there. Then we had our actress read her lines into a recorder. In editing, her beautiful face was shown to best advantage, while her taped lines were edited over the townsfolk's reactions.

Poorly Scheduled Light Plot Setup   If intricate light plots and setups have been scheduled for the beginning of a shooting day, you can count on one or even two hours' delay. Once these two hours are wasted, it is impossible to catch up. If you are faced with an intricate light plot:

• Set up the day *before* the scheduled shot.

- Set up the day of the shot, but film at a different area of your location while the setup takes place.

Lack of Alternate Locations   Shooting outdoors, you may lose precious time if you are rained out. One rainy day may ruin your entire location schedule. Therefore, make every effort to have an alternate interior location available, but also make certain that you will be charged for it only if you actually film at the alternate location.

How to Bring in a Motion Picture on Budget and on Time

The Director Has Done His or Her Homework   After the director has, together with the writer, restructured the script and written the shooting script, the script supervisor will join them. Now is the time to start on the various breakdowns. (I am not referring to nervous breakdowns; those will probably loom on the horizon as the shooting date approaches and so many things still need to be done.)

By now locations have been consolidated, omitted, or changed, and the shooting script has been marked with take numbers. You are ready to write:

Location list
Scene breakdown
Story board
Setup list/shot list

It is beneficial for the script supervisor and the director to work closely together. If you, the director, involve yourself with the breakdown *now,* you will have a much better handle on the film once shooting starts.

Location List   First you will consolidate all scenes taking place in a specific location. Determine which of the scenes will be *day* shots and which *night* shots.

Scene Breakdown   (Continuity List) The continuity breakdown lists all information necessary for a scene to be shot. Below is an example of a breakdown sheet.

SCRIPT SUPERVISOR'S BREAKDOWN SHEET (Continuity)

TITLE: *Alms for the Past*

SHOOTING DATES: August 18, 1990

SCENE NUMBER: 19   DAY: X   NIGHT: PAGES: 35   TIME: 4 hrs

SET: INTERIOR/EXTERIOR: INTERIOR/Chris kitchen

SYNOPSIS:

Chris, unpacking, hears some strange sounds outside the house. There is a supernatural happening, a cup flies off the counter and crashes against the kitchen wall.

Ellen arrives, she introduces herself as Seymor's wife and invites Chris to a party. Chris tries to find out about the owner of the house—Inez—and the strange happenings she encountered the day before.

CAST	WARDROBE	PROPS
Ellen	Cotton dress	Bags and groceries,
Chris	Robe	teakettle, tea-bags,
		etc., tea-cups
		Duplicate cups for
		special effect

VEHICLES AND ANIMALS	EFFECTS	
	Cup crashing	
	against kitchen wall	
	(camera: slow	
	motion)	
	Have duplicate	
	cups handy	

SOUND	BITS AND EXTRAS	CONTINUITY
Knock on door		
Sound as cup		
crashes against wall		
Rustling sound from		
outside		
Footsteps		

SCRIPT SUPERVISOR: _____

SCRIPT SUPERVISOR'S BREAKDOWN SHEET (Continuity)

TITLE: *Jungle Trap*

SHOOTING DATES: August, 1990

SCENE NUMBER: 19　DAY:　NIGHT: X　PAGES: 56, 57　TIME: 4 hrs

SET: INTERIOR/EXTERIOR: INTERIOR/Hotel, Chris's room

SYNOPSIS:

Oby shows Chris to her room in the hotel. This scene gives the first indication of the "otherworldliness" of the place.

CAST	WARDROBE	PROPS
Chris Oby	Khaki outfit Tropical helmet Bellman's outfit	Chris shoulder bag Duffel bag Toilet articles on dressing table Shirts, slacks Dollar bill
VEHICLES None	**EFFECTS** Shrunken head Chair that rocks by itself	
SOUND Laughter	**BITS AND EXTRAS** None	**CONTINUITY**

SCRIPT SUPERVISOR: _____

Shot List and Camera Setup List   The continuity list leads to the creation of the shot and setup lists. Depending on the situation, you may be able to write both lists during the preproduction period. At times, unfortunately, you will be forced to write these important lists on the evening prior to shooting. Make certain that you discuss these lists with your cinematographer. Don't try to do without these lists. During shooting you will be under severe pressure, and without the lists you will be prone to forget one or more takes. Moreover, it is according to your setup lists that the cinematographer and gaffer will arrive at a correct light plot.

As you take another look at the shooting script, you will notice that each take has been numbered. Writing your shooting list, you will assemble all numbers that take place at one certain place in the scene, regardless of whether these segments will be shown in sequence.

For example, referring back to the shot list for *Jungle Trap* (see page 28), you will find four camera setups.

- Camera setup I: Facing door, left from Chris and Oby
- Camera setup II: At the dressing table
- Camera setup III: Hand-held on Oby
- Camera setup IV: At the bed

Story Board   For complicated scenes you may wish to use a *story board,* a series of small drawings that show the way your actors move and the way each segment leads into the next.

Do not confuse a story board with a *breakdown board.* The breakdown board is for the producer's use only. The information in the continuity breakdown has been transferred to a board via individually colored cardboard strips. Fortunately, the breakdown board is not your responsibility.

Production Report   Every evening your production manager (or your script supervisor) will hand in a production report. This report lists the entire activity of each shooting day. Make certain that the production report has been kept meticulously, as it contains some important information about added or deleted lines.

Raw Stock   Carefully estimate how much raw stock you will require for every scene.

Cover Shots   Don't forget to cover yourself with a number of CUs.

Actors   Use skilled motion picture actors only.

Crew   Use skilled key personnel only.

Equipment

- Check your equipment thoroughly before shooting.
- Discuss all equipment needs with the cinematographer. Too much equipment requires more crew and prolongs your setup time; too little equipment may cause delays.
- Take advantage of weekend rental rates.

Setup Time

- Do not waste time by setting up a scene requiring an intricate light plot first thing in the morning. If possible, have this scene set up the day before.
- Try to set up less complicated scenes while you are shooting at a different part of your location.
- Schedule setup time wisely.
- Use unavoidable setup delays to rehearse with your actors.

Locations

- Consolidate locations if possible.
- Minimize travel time between locations.
- Rent an expensive location for one or two days only.
- Set up a reasonable shooting schedule and *stick with it.*

Actors   Use *skilled motion picture actors* only. (These actors do not have to be members of the Screen Actors Guild but they have to be *camera trained.*)

The Director's Homework

Last but not least, a short, comprehensive look at the director's homework that—if done properly—will bring in your motion picture on time and on budget:

- Agree with your writer on the final script. Structure the final script, and if possible participate in any rewrites.
- Write the shooting script.
- Familiarize yourself with those areas of the budget that are your direct responsibility.
- Together with the cinematographer and art director, look for locations. Procure the producer's approval for the selected locations.
- Make certain that the producer has arranged for sufficient liability and equipment insurance.
- Rehearse with actors.
- Together with the script supervisor write the continuity breakdown.
- Work on the shot and setup lists. Discuss these lists with your cinematographer.
- Keep track of setup times and use these wisely.
- Each evening, check the production report and review next day's shooting schedule.
- Each day, view dailies.
- *Always expect the unexpected.* Face every problem that arises with a smile and say, "No problem at all."

Part Two

3.

Motion Pictures:

A

Visual Art

You, the motion picture director, are going to tell a story. You decide how you will relate your story to the audience, and how the audience will *see* it—that is, you'll utilize the powers of the camera to tell your story. But beware; do not decide on a certain camera move or an interesting shot because of its creative value. You have a story to tell, remember? The audience, as disappointing as this sounds, should never be aware of your creative prowess. It is your responsibility to grip the audience, to make them participate in the story you tell. Think about this for a moment: as you read a novel, do you want to admire the writer's elegant use of words, or do you want to know what is going on now and what will happen next? The same applies to a motion picture. Neither do you expect—or desire—to be awed by great acting techniques or incredible camera moves; you go to the theater to see a story unfold.

The Audience's Point of View

First you'll have to decide: from what *emotional point of view* should the audience see what is happening on the screen? As we have discussed previously, a writer is concerned mostly with creating a story via dialog and characters' actions, while you as director will bring it to life via effective camera setups and movements. (Needless to say, effective camera work, which makes *the story interesting* to the audience, won't increase your budget one penny if you have decided on camera setups *before* shooting begins.)

The term *point of view* refers not to the story's theme but to the *position* you want the audience to take while watching the story. This may be either the *omnipotent* position (a viewer who knows everything and sees everything) or the *character's* position. For the audience to be in the omnipotent position, the director will give equal importance to all incidents and to all characters, and will show actions from the hero's as well as the villain's point of view. If the audience is to be in the character's position, then it will see what the character observes and will participate in that character's emotions.

SCENE USING OMNIPOTENT POSITION

Interior Kathy's House. Hallway. Night.

302 *(On the door. We hear a slight scratching noise; it seems a passkey has been inserted. Slowly, ever so slowly, the door opens, and a* BURGLAR *slips in. He seems to be familiar with the place. Quickly he opens the hallway closet and hides.)*

303 **Interior Hallway Closet. Night.**

*(*BURGLAR *slips out a knife, waits; we hear the front door opening.)*

304 **Hallway. Night.**

*(*KATHY *enters. She takes off her coat and is ready to open the hallway closet, when a spot on the coat sleeve catches her attention.)*

KATHY: Got to go to the dry cleaner's.

*(*KATHY *throws the coat into a corner, then proceeds to the living room.)*

305 **Interior Hallway Closet. Night.**

*(*BURGLAR *waits for a beat, then, knife poised, he exits the closet.)*

So far, so good—assuming that Kathy, the karate expert, saves herself. Now we will proceed by placing the audience in the character's (hero's) position.

SCENE USING CHARACTER'S POSITION

Exterior Kathy's House. Night.

302 *(KATHY approaches. Nervously she opens her purse, hunts for her keys.*

303 *CU on her hands searching for the key. She cannot find it.*

304 *Back on KATHY. She looks over her shoulder to see if someone has followed her.*

305 *KATHY's POV. The deserted street.*

306 *Back on KATHY. She hunts through her coat pockets, finds the key, and opens the front door.)*

Interior Kathy's House. Night.

307 **Interior Hallway. Night.**

(On KATHY entering. She slams the door shut.

308 *CU hands shaking as she locks and bolts the door.*

309 *On KATHY. She turns on the light switch, looks around, sighs a sigh of relief. She takes off her coat. Pan with KATHY as she walks to the hallway closet, is ready to open it, but notices a spot on the coat sleeve.)*

KATHY: Got to go to the dry cleaner's.

(She throws the coat into a corner. Pan with KATHY as she proceeds to the living room.)

Interior Living Room. Night.

310 *(Pan with KATHY as she walks to her desk and lights a lamp. Pull In as she leans down to pick up some files.*

322 *Reverse on KATHY, Pull In more to Tight Medium as a hand clamps her mouth shut and a knife touches her neck.)*

VO* BURGLAR: They told me you had the file.

Looking at the two scenes (telling the same story in a different way), you can see why you should decide on the audience's point of view *before* you start shooting. Your decision has to be made while you write your shooting script.

---

*Voice-over.

CREATING EXPECTATION

Second, you will have to be concerned about planting certain expectations in your audience's mind. Take the following scene, for instance:

504 **Exterior Elementary School. Day.**
(KATHY *enters the building.*)
505 **Interior Elementary School. Hallway. Day.**
(KATHY *enters the principal's office.*)

If you show Kathy entering the buliding and then pan with her as she walks toward the principal's office, the audience expects nothing out of the ordinary to happen. If, however, Kathy has been summoned to a conference (her first job is on the line) and she is apprehensive, you should let the audience *know* about it. In this case the scene should be shot as follows:

404 **Exterior Elementary School. Day.**
(KATHY *enters the building.*)
405 **Interior Elementary School. Hallway. Day.**
(*Pan with* KATHY *as she approaches the principal's office. At the door she hesitates.*)
406 **Interior Elementary School. Day.**
(*Medium Shot on the glass-paneled door. On* KATHY *looking in. After hesitating for a beat, she opens the door.*)

Granted, the second interpretation of the scene is the more interesting one, but *only* if you want to show Kathy's apprehension.

Easy, isn't it? All you have to do is decide what you want the audience to experience. Alfred Hitchcock, the master of suspense, employed the character position point of view to the apex in his film *Rear Window,* when a wheelchair-bound James Stewart watches Grace Kelly searching the suspected murderer's apartment. The camera *never* takes in Grace Kelly's point of view; it shows only what James Stewart observes through his binoculars. Immediately the audience, experiencing the search through James Stewart's eyes as he sees the killer approaching, gets caught in the terror of his helplessness.

EDITING IN THE CAMERA

Your last, equally important, concern is "editing in the camera." As discussed previously, the traditional way of shooting a Master Shot, Two-Shot, Reversals, and Closeups is time consuming, expensive, and sometimes pedestrian. You will do much better to edit in the camera. Therefore you must edit as you write your shooting script. Unquestionably the statement "The foundation of film art is editing" holds as much truth today as it did when Pudovkin first stated it in 1933.*

The Eleven Basic Shots

And now we will take a look at the admittedly complicated choices of camera setup and moves you will use to create a film:

1. Establishing Shot
2. Master Shot
3. Full Shot
4. ¾ or Hollywood Shot
5. Medium Shot
    a. Two-Shot
    b. Walking Two-Shot
    c. Standing Two-Shot
    d. Reversal
    e. Over-the-Shoulder Shot
    f. Telephone Conversation
6. Closeup
7. Tilt
8. Pan Shot
9. Tracking Shot
10. Cutaway Shot
11. Pull In/Pull Out

---

*Pudovkin, Vsevolod, *Film Technique,* Newness, London 1933, p. 170.

I know this looks overwhelming at first glance, but these eleven shots are the *basis of directing*. You, the beginning director, must master them, in the very same way you mastered your multiplication table. There is no easy way out—sorry!

Each shot has been labeled for easy reference on the following pages. As you move on to the more complicated ones, I have added demonstration scenes. You may easily adapt the camera setups and moves given in each example to the film you are directing.

And now, let's get to work!

1. Establishing Shot

(Long Shot)

The Establishing Shot serves two purposes:

- It shows the general environment (city street, seashore, etc.)
- It shows a character in juxtaposition to that environment (lone man walking down a deserted street).

2. Master Shot

The Master Shot, very much like a filmed stage play, shows the entire scene in a Full Shot. There are no camera moves, Medium Shots, or CUs. At times a Master Shot serves to acquaint the audience with the characters participating in a scene (camera moves and various angles will come later), or it simply serves as a blueprint for the editor. Unless you are shooting a large group scene, avoid a Master Shot. It is too time consuming.

3. Full Shot

A Full Shot establishes an actor from head to toe. You may Pull In or cut from an Establishing Shot to a Full Shot in order to establish your characters' positions more clearly.

4. ¾, or Hollywood, Shot

The ¾ Shot shows an actor down to the knees. Used by directors during the 1930s, this shot is less popular today. But if you are forced to shoot within the confines of a small area, you may as well use it to establish the environment before cutting to a Two-Shot.

5. Medium Shot

The actor is the center of attention, seen from either the waist or hip up. In a moving Medium Shot the hipline shot is best, while a static shot should concentrate on the actor from the waist up. The Medium Shot has these six variations:

Two-Shot
Walking Two-Shot
Standing Two-Shot
Reversal
Over-the-Shoulder Shot
Telephone Conversation

TWO-SHOT

In a Two-Shot two actors are sitting, standing, or walking next to each other. Take great care to frame a Two-Shot correctly:

- Do not show too much headroom.
- Conversely, do not frame a Two-Shot too loosely, or you will be faced with unattractively wide sidelines.
- Because TV will cut off some of your sidelines, leave enough space so as not to have your actors partially cut off.

Next to framing, a Two-Shot presents some other problems for the unwary director:

Positioned (seating or standing) next to his partner, actor *A* obviously has to look at actress *B* while *B* is delivering her lines. Most likely both actors will turn *en profile* while engaged in a dialog. Granted that the two beautiful people just paid off their last installment on their respective nose jobs and the profiles seen on the screen are perfect, nevertheless the fact remains: profile shots are ineffective because they *do not show an actor's emotion.* Only eyes and mouth convey emotions, while the static line of forehead-nose-chin does not. In a two-shot an actor's face ought to be seen halfway between profile and *en face* (frontal facial position), at a 45-degree angle. This way the viewer will see at least some eye and mouth movements.

Once a 45-degree angle has been set, watch the eye line. If actor *A* is taller than actress *B, A* has to look down and *B* has to look up.

Since any dialog shot in a Two-Shot appears static by nature, actors should be encouraged to *face* the camera every so often. This, of course, should be done in a natural, never forced, way:

- During the actor's lines.
- While listening to a partner.
- During silent (reflective) moments.

I admit, all of the above seems a little complicated. But don't worry, any skilled motion picture actor who is well versed in on-camera techniques won't have any difficulty with Two-Shots.*

WALKING TWO-SHOT

The same on-camera acting techniques apply to the seated or Walking Two-Shot. In addition, actors should be made aware that they have to walk together closely on a straight line, and avoid wobbling or weaving back and forth. Often during a Walking Two-Shot actors are required to stop, continue their dialog, and then move on. Here are some points you may advise your actors about:

How to Audition for Movies and TV, by Renée Harmon (New York: Walker & Co, 1992), will give you a clear enumeration of motion picture acting techniques.

- Move into your Reversal Shot (see page 65) smoothly by counting how many steps you will have to take to hit your mark.
- Move out of your Reversal smoothly by stepping out on the foot closest to the camera.
- Know where your marks are. Do not omit or add any dialog, since the grips pulling the camera depend on your hitting your mark *precisely* and/or stopping or commencing to walk on a specific *word*.

STANDING TWO-SHOT

Whenever you are faced with a lengthy, possibly boring but necessary exposition through dialog, you'll choose a Walking Two-Shot. Whenever you do not have the space for one, then you may do well to decide upon a Standing Two-Shot and *move your actors around*.

A Standing Two-Shot looks more natural if you place actor *A* (Archie) facing the camera and actor *B* (Babs) in a 45-degree profile position.

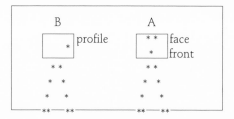

The following scene provides an example of a Standing Two-Shot:

Interior Archie's Living Room. Night.

687   (ARCHIE, *facing camera, waits for* BABS *impatiently.*)

ARCHIE: I have ordered the limo for precisely seven o'clock . . .

(BABS, *in full evening attire, walks into the frame. She stops close to* ARCHIE *positioned at a 45-degree angle.*)

ARCHIE: You know how angry my parents are whenever we're late.

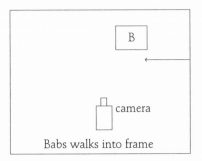

BABS: Too bad. Let them wait.

(Pan with BABS as she walks to an antique chest of drawers. She picks up her evening bag, and looking into the mirror, she adjusts her hair.)

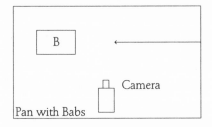

BABS: They have nothing else to do. You better be glad that I agreed . . .

(Archie walks into frame.)

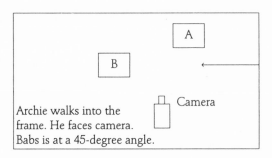

BABS: . . . to spend a boring evening with those two ancients.

(Now both are in a Two-Shot and the argument begins.)

REVERSAL

In a Reversal Shot two actors are *facing* each other. Reversals should present no difficulties if you have worked them out during your homework session. Just as in the Two-Shot, it is important that actors *do not* look at each other. Have actor A look at actress B's ear that is closest to the camera, and vice versa. You will shoot actor A's lines while actress B delivers her lines off-camera. Then you will go through the same process with actress B. This is not quite as easy as it may sound, but being forewarned about some hurdles, you should have no difficulties:

- Shoot plenty of reaction shots and VOs (voice-overs) of the actors' lines.
- Remind your actors to take two beats (each beat consists of counting "one thousand and one") before answering their partners. Later you will need this time lapse for smooth editing.

In a Reversal Shot you have to keep the direction consistent. If actor A looked to the *right,* he must look to the *left* in the Reversal Shot. Actress B, who looked to the *left,* must look to the *right* in the Reversal. Both actors, though actually looking in opposite directions, will *seem* to look at each other. If you keep this simple rule in mind, you will save yourself much trouble later on during the editing process.

Theoretically, for each of the Reversal Shots the lighting has to be adjusted and the camera has to be moved—as we all know, a time-consuming business. Well, not necessarily: if actor A has been placed in front of a desk and a window, it is obvious that actress B's position is the fourth or open wall, the spot where the camera stands. Leave lights and camera where they are. Do not set up anew, but have your grips bring in a flat and one or two appropriate props (make certain these have *not* been established previously), and shoot actress B in actor A's position.

There are a few things you want to remember as you edit a Reversal:

- Watch the rhythm of the scene. The cuts on each actor should be *unequal* in duration.
- Do not cut: actor *A* talks, actress *B* talks, but at times place actor *A*'s reaction shot on actor *B*'s VO for more interesting transitions.

OVER-THE-SHOULDER SHOT

The Over-the-Shoulder Shot is a Reversal Shot taken over the partner's shoulder. If actor *A* has been established at camera left, he must *remain* camera left in his Over-the-Shoulder Shot.

TELEPHONE CONVERSATIONS

Even though a telephone conversation takes place on two different locations, it is imperative that actors are placed in such a way as to *face each other*.

6. Closeup

The Closeup (CU) is your most powerful tool:

- Medium CU is most effective for dialog.
- Head-and-shoulder CU brings the audience closer to the character. Take care that your actor neither stiffens (shows no emotion) nor indicates (expresses emotions too strongly) for CU.

- The critical CU shows the actor's face only. It is perfect for
  moments requiring the expression of thoughts and feelings, but is
  less effective for dialog.

Sometimes you may do well to shoot your leading lady's CU first, before shooting Two-Shots and Reversals, as long as she is still fresh and her makeup hasn't caked.

Since you, the beginning director, will have your eyes on rental video distribution (the small screen), you may go more extensively for CU and Medium Shot variations, but do not be tempted to use CUs haphazardly. A CU ought to be used for:

- Reaction shots.
- Highly emotional shots.
- Shots that will give maximum impact to your story.
- Transitional shots from one scene to the next.
- Bridging awkward moments in editing.
- Ambience shots, to add mood to an environment.

7. Tilt

The camera moves in a vertical arch. You may either Tilt Up or Tilt Down. Tilts should be executed with great care. All jerky movements have to be avoided.

8. Pan Shot

The camera moves in a horizontal arc. Lead, don't follow, when panning — that is, the camera moves *ahead* of the actor. Avoid Swish Pans — the rapid movement from one subject to another — unless the Swish Pan makes an *emotional statement.*

9. Tracking Shot

The camera moves either forward or backward. As discussed previously, building track for a moving shot (Tracking Shot) is time consuming and expensive. So why not rent a wheelchair, knowing that your camera director has a steady hand, and trust your grip to push the wheelchair? Your Tracking Shots will be just as effective. Tracking Shots are commonly used for Walking Two-Shots, when actors have to explain some background information. Your audience will take more kindly to such exposition if it takes place at an interesting spot such as a park, shopping mall, or art gallery.

10. Cutaway Shot

Cutaway Shots cutting from one subject to the next are important for matching of shots and transitions.

11. Pull In/Pull Out

These shots pull in or out on an actor or an object, and follow in *continuity with what has happened previously in a scene.*

Now let's move on to the following on-screen directions, which also have much to do with continuity of movement.

Center line
Screen directions
Matching of shots (Overlap)
Transitions
Framing

Center Line

Much has been written, and many have worried, about this nemesis called the center line (or gray line or imaginary line). But if you keep in mind that the center line determines screen direction, and therefore all camera setups have to be placed on the *same side* of the center line, the concept becomes less intimidating.

Let me explain:

Actors *A* and *B* move into frame in a ¾ Shot. From there they have a dialog in a Medium Shot, followed by CUs. If the camera has been placed *in front* of the actors for the ¾ Shot, it has to be placed *in front* of the actors for the Medium Shot and CUs. If you decide to place the camera behind the actors or on either side of them for the Medium Shot, then *a new center line has been established,* and you'll have to shoot the ¾ Shot as well as the CUs from this newly established position. In other words, during the editing process you cannot cut from a ¾ Shot, where the camera has been set up in front of the actors, to a Medium Shot, where the camera has been set up to the right of actor *A*. Whenever you reposition your camera, a new center line has been established.

This does not, however, imply that the camera should never cross the center line. In a scene featuring a group of actors the camera will have to cross the center line every so often. The transit from one center line to the next is achieved by a *Cutaway CU.*

You won't have any difficulties with center lines if you stick to two simple formulas:

- Consecutive takes (¾ to Medium, Medium to CU) have to be shot from the *same* camera setup.
- If, because of the composition of a scene, you'll have to cross the center line, and thus establish a new center line, you'll have to use a CU to *bridge* the transition.

Correct center lines (will work for editing)

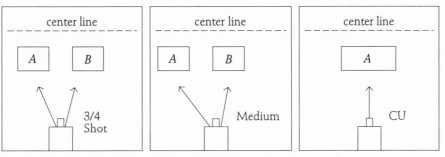

All shots are taken from the same *camera position.*

Unless you use a bridging CU, do *not* cross the center line:

Incorrect center lines (will not work for editing)

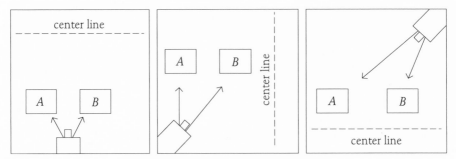

Different camera setups create new center lines.

Screen Directions

Screen directions apply to the correlation of camera setup and actor movement. You'll have to observe the center line, but you should face no difficulties if you keep in mind that *regardless of change of location,* camera setups always have to be on the already established side of the actor. That is, if you start a scene with the camera positioned to the right of the actor, all subsequent camera setups must be to the actor's right. If you desire to change screen direction, make a transition with a neutral shot, and show your subject frontal.

No problem, right? For the purpose of illustration, let's look at a scene that takes Jack from the office building's hallway to Mr. Marvin's office.*

CAMERA SETUP	SCENE NUMBER	ACTION
1. (To JACK's *right at foot of stairs.*	204	**Office Building. Hallway.** (JACK *descends the stairs. He worries about seeing his boss.)*
Pan with JACK.*)*		

*From *Red Satchel* (Ciara Productions, 1990).

Stairs⟶

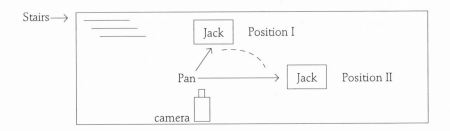

2. *(Frontal setup. Neutral. Tracking Shot.)*

205

Different Area Hallway. Day.
(On JACK *walking.)*

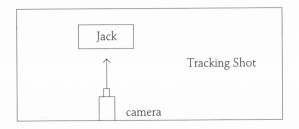

3. *(To* JACK's *left. Pan with* JACK, *as he walks to door. Hold on* JACK. *Change of screen direction. Change of center line.)*

206

In Front of Mr. Marvin's Office. Day.
*(*JACK *approaches the door, takes a deep breath, and enters.)*

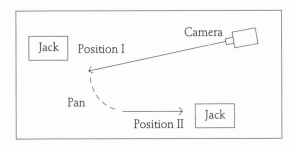

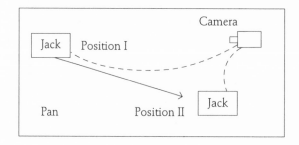

4. *(To* JACK's *left. Over* MR.   207   **Mr. Marvin's Office.**
   MARVIN's *shoulder on* JACK   **Day.**
   entering. Same center line.)   *(Head held high, a smile on*
                                                   lips, JACK *enters and*
                                                   approaches MR. MARVIN's
                                                   desk.)

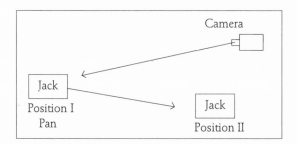

Directional shots that involve a number of different locations, and consequently different camera setups, can become confusing unless you have set up your shots (and directionals) ahead of the shooting.

Now let's assume that half hidden behind a door, Samantha—the villain—is watching our hero. Her looks have to follow screen direction, too:

205 **Office Building. Hallway. Day.**
   (On JACK *walking.*
206 *A door opens a little and* SAMANTHA *peeks out. She looks over her* left
   shoulder.

207 *On* JACK *walking. Without noticing* SAMANTHA, *he passes by her office.*
208 *On* SAMANTHA. *She opens the door a little wider. Looking over her* right
     shoulder, *she smiles her evil smile.)*

Matching of Shots

(Overlap)

Considering the fact that you are editing in the camera, don't ever forget to
overlap from one camera angle to the next. In other words, an overlap (match)
is the transition between shots that depict the same action. Two simple rules
are:

1. Always *cut on motion.*
2. Always *overlap* action as much as possible.

In an overlap (match) it is important to shoot the action *past* the point
where it will be cut in the editing process, and *begin* the second angle with
part of the action executed before the cut. This way the editor will have no
difficulty matching the two angles, and the movement will flow smoothly
and naturally. Great care should be exercised so that everything—facial
expression; placement of props, hands, and head—will be *identical* in both
angles. Take a good look at the following:

¾ Shot	745	**Country Road. Day.**
		(JONATHAN *approaches. Suddenly something catches his attention. He bends down.*
Medium Shot	746	*He bends down more.*
CU	747	JONATHAN's *POV: a glittering object.*
Tight Medium	748	*He picks up the object and begins to rise.*
¾ Shot	749	*His eyes on the object,* JONATHAN *straightens.)*

Take 746 cuts back to some of the bending movement of 745. Take 749
must be started with Jonathan's hand in the same position as in take 748.

Overlap is important in a pickup. At times a scene works fine up to a certain point only, and the director decides to pick up from there. Remember that you have to begin your second take before the point where you had to cut.

Regardless of how diligently you work on matching your takes, the danger lurks that an overlap may not work. The wise director makes certain to have enough Cutaway Shots (CU of faces, objects, etc.) to bridge any awkward moments.

Transitions

The basic purpose of a transitional shot is to:

- Transit from one camera position to the next (crossing the center line).
- Transit from one picture size to the next (never cut from a Full Shot to a CU, but always transit with a Medium Shot).
- To bridge action from one location to another.

To bridge from one location to the next is probably the most cumbersome of all transitions. Don't ever try to follow one picture size with an *identical* one, unless you *show action in motion* (Pull In/Pull Out). For instance, do not follow Tracy's CU as she sighs longingly with the CU of a beach ball in someone's hands. But consider these shots:

8 *(Medium Shot on* TRACY *sighing longingly. Pull In to CU on* TRACY.
9 *CU on beach ball being tossed into the air. Tilt Up with movement.*
10 *Pull Back to ¾ Shot as ball descends.)*

Even though the CU on the beach ball does follow Tracy's CU, both takes will cut, since—because of the Pull In and Pull Out—the transition is not static but shows action in motion.

In the next example we are again faced with two Establishing Shots featuring the same picture size. Here is the kind of transition you *want to avoid:*

Airport Terminal. Day.

674 *(Establishing Shot of terminal.* LAURA *walks into the frame. Pan with her as she walks to a window and looks out.)*

675 **Airport Tarmac. Day.**

  *(*LAURA's *POV, the tarmac, Establishing Shot.)*

Boring, right? So why not work a little harder, and come up with this:

Airport Terminal. Day.

674 *(¾ Shot on* LAURA *walking. Pull In to Medium Shot.*

675 *Medium Shot [frontal] on* LAURA *walking [shot used to change directions].*

676 *Pull Back to a ¾ Shot and Pan with* LAURA *as she approaches a window. Hold on her as she looks out.)*

  Airport Tarmac. Day.

677 *(*LAURA's *POV, Establishing Shot of tarmac.)*

If you're in a pinch, just changing the picture size should provide you with a satisfactory transition.

305 **Downtown Los Angeles. Day.**

  (Establishing Shot of busy downtown street.)

306 **Golf Course. Day.**

  (¾ Shot of RALPH *happily swinging his golf club.)*

I'm certain you've got the picture. Effective transitions are not difficult to achieve if you consider the *logical flow* of your motion picture. Here are some basic suggestions:

- Either: begin each scene with a static camera, and have your subjects move.
  Or: begin each scene with a moving camera, and have your subjects static.
- Use CU to bridge from one scene to the next.
- Vary picture size from one scene to the next.
- Pull In on one scene, Pull Out on the following scene (action in motion).

- In addition use sound effects, natural sound, and music for transitional purposes.

Framing

When we speak about framing, we speak about the composition of a frame. In other words, we speak about the pictorial aspects of a motion picture—lines that are pleasing to the audience's eyes without disturbing the story to be told. Clearly, a movie's visual composition should *strengthen* whatever the director wants the audience to observe. All of the above, I agree, sounds rather theoretical, but it is easy to achieve if you remember the following:

BOUNDARIES

Each frame (picture) has four boundaries and is divided into thirds. Let's take, for instance, the Establishing Shot of a suburban street. The pavement and a group of skateboarding children (they provide the necessary movement to the scene) occupy one third, and trees and horizon round off your composition. A tree trunk situated to the far right of your frame provides the focal point that pulls the picture together.

FRAMING PROPS

(Smaller Objects)

Framing props are important for the composition of a Medium Shot. These are used to draw the audience's attention to the *middle of the frame*. Framing props and/or objects should neither *distract* the audience nor *overpower* the actor. Do not position them in such a way that—unexpectedly—a vase seems to grow on your leading lady's head.

PLACING ACTORS

To place your actress *in the middle* of the frame is a poor choice. Always position her *slightly* to either side. Also, do not place your actor *too close to the boundary* of your frame, unless something happens behind him.

SIDELINES

Always be aware of the safe action area, also called the "television cutoff" —the part of the frame that will have to be cut off as the 35mm film is transferred to videotape. For this reason be sure to leave enough open space on either side of the frame. Be especially aware of the necessary open space when working on moving camera shots.

You, the beginning director, should never take framing lightly. Proper framing, as each shot moves into the next, is the basis for the effective sequencing of a motion picture.

Difficult Setups Made a Little Easier

We all have seen movies that unexpectedly begin to drag. This static quality often happens, one has to conclude, as soon as the director is faced with group scenes:

Table scene
Three-character scene
Large group scene
Four-character scene
Fight scene

Now let's find ways to make these admittedly difficult scenes a little easier to shoot.

Generally you ought to avoid a Master Shot, but a group scene does require one. Fortunately, the Master Shot does *not* have to be perfect. Never mind if an actor fluffs a line, or the sound of a lawn mower disrupts a tender love scene. Let the camera roll, go on shooting. The Master Shot serves only as a *road map* for you, the director. It informs the audience as to the characters involved, and it reminds you, the director, of your characters' physical position in the scene, information you will need later on as you edit the respective Two-Shots, CUs, and Reversals. Always remember, the Master Shot as filmed will *never* be seen on the screen.

For all group scenes keep the following in mind:

- Disregard the center line.
- Watch eye lines and opposing looks.
- Compose your picture *asymmetrically* rather then symmetrically.
- If possible, move your actors *and* your camera.
- Shoot plenty of cover CU to bridge as you cross center lines.
- Have lively interchanges among all characters. This may require some revision of your shooting script.

TABLE SCENE

This diagram shows a static four-character scene. All characters are seated in a restaurant booth. This suggests built-in difficulties, as there is no other way to position the actors than symmetrically.

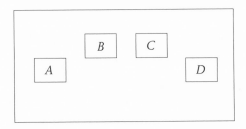

Limiting the dialog between *B* and *C*, *A* and *D*, or *A* and *B* will only add boredom to a static scene. If, however, you strive for a lively interchange:

A and *C*
D and *B*

C and *A*
B and *A*
C and *D*

and vary your picture sizes between Medium Shots and CUs, you will come up with a visually enjoyable scene.

THREE-CHARACTER SCENE

A three-character scene is most effective if both camera and actors keep moving.

315 **Interior Casino, Las Vegas.**
(*On roulette wheel CU, we hear music, laughter, and the click of the roulette ball.*)

316 **Interior Claudia's Dressing Room. Night.**
(CLAUDIA, *a gorgeous show girl, sits at her dressing table. Medium Shot.*)

CLAUDIA: I know my career is on the skids.

(*Pull Back to include* RALPH, *her boyfriend.* AL, *her manager, a wiry, nervous man, enters the frame.*)

AL: You have not one offer. Once your Las Vegas stint . . .

(AL *begins pacing. Pan with him.*)

AL: . . . is over. We have to do . . .

(*Pan with* AL *as he approaches* RALPH. *Hold on* RALPH *and* AL.)

AL: . . . something about Claudia's career.

Take a good look at the *Red Satchel* scene, and you will discover:

315 (*Commences with the CU of the roulette wheel.*
316 *Changes picture size from CU to Medium Shot. It uses sound as transitory device. Pull-Back and Pull-In as well as Pan Shots give movement to the scene.*)

If for any reason—such as time or space limitations—this scene had to be kept static, and since there is no good reason to intercut CUs, you'd have to concentrate your efforts on positioning your actors in interesting ways. Diagrammed, the scene might look like this (the arrow indicates the direction of looks):

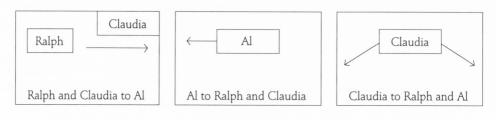

However, if you wish to show the trio's frustration about Claudia's failing career, bring more *movement* to the scene, such as in the example following.

(Pull Out.

AL: Your name has to become a household word again.

Pan with AL *as he walks toward* CLAUDIA *and* RALPH.

AL: Your name has to be in print . . .

On AL, CLAUDIA, RALPH.

RALPH: . . . on TV.

AL: Right, so how about my . . .

Pan with CLAUDIA. *She turns, faces* RALPH.

CLAUDIA: . . . insane suggestion?

On RALPH *and* AL.

RALPH: How about it?

CLAUDIA *(VO):* Why should I become the victim . . .

On CLAUDIA.

CLAUDIA: . . . of a dumb, no . . .

Pan with CLAUDIA *as she walks to her dressing table.*

CLAUDIA: . . . outrageously stupid— and dangerous—jewelry heist.

AL *enters frame, he leans across her dressing table. Medium Shot.*

AL: I'll arrange everything . . .

RALPH *enters frame from the opposite side.*

RALPH: . . . reporters . . .

On CLAUDIA. *Suddenly beaming, she looks up.*

CLAUDIA: Paparazzi.

CU on her radiant smile.)

LARGE GROUP SCENES

If you shoot large group scenes, you will do well to divide your group into segments of two, three, and four characters, and permit the scene to develop in an ever-shifting, kaleidoscopic manner. Whether you choose the three-camera setup or the traditional setup (Full Shot, Medium Shot, CU) is immaterial, so long as you arrive at a lively visual pattern and have plenty of CUs for bridging. Like the fight scene, the group scene cannot be edited in the camera. Here is an example from our "satchel throwing" scene.

(Full Shot.

Hotel Lobby. Day.
(On everyone. Three satchels are thrown and tossed, caught and thrown again.)

DR. MEEK *(screams):* A bomb . . .

Medium Shot, various angles.

(On everyone, vary between designated groups.

CU.

On satchel.

Medium.

On hands.

Pull Back.

On LIL. *Frightened, she holds on to the satchel. Finally, screaming, she tosses it.*

Swish Pan.

On hands and arms, catching and tossing three satchels.)

CU.

BILLY BOB: Run . . . run . . .

Medium Shot.

SHEIK: The bomb explodes at midnight.

Medium Shot, different angle.	OLD LADY: That's better than bingo.
	(She tosses the satchel.)
Medium, different angle.	BARBIE: I'm going to faint.
	(Sound: The clock strikes one.
CU.	*On clock, it is almost midnight. The clock strikes two.*
Flashes, all different angles:	
CU	*Red satchel.*
CU	MEEK's *face.*
Medium	SHEIK *tosses satchel. Sound of clock, strikes three, four.*
CU	*On clock, strikes five.*
CU	BARBIE.
CU	OLD LADY.
CU.	*The clock strikes five, six, seven.*
Medium.	*On hands tossing satchel. The clock strikes eight.*
Various angles.	*On satchels being tossed. The clock strikes nine.*
CU.	*The satchel lands in someone's hands.*
Pull Back to Medium.	*A minister, smiling calmly, holds one of the red satchels.)*
	MINISTER: Good evening, I hope I'm not interrupting anything. *(The clock strikes ten, eleven.*
¾ Shot.	*On the group, catatonic. They stare at the minister.* BARBIE *holds a satchel; so does the* SHEIK. *The clock strikes twelve. Sound of explosion.*

Cut to SHEIK, *Medium.*

Face blackened but otherwise alive, the SHEIK *shakes his head sadly.)*

FOUR-CHARACTER SCENE

And now we will look at another scene (the arrest scene from *Red Satchel*) that proved tricky because it had to be shot within a limited area. This scene adhered to the center line, and there was *no* possibility for the actors to move. Consequently we depended on rather short takes and Pull In/Pull Out. Here is the setup of the scene:

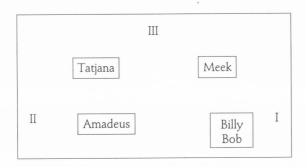

¾ *Shot.*

Park. Exterior. Day.
(On DR. MEEK, *looking around. Apparently he is waiting for someone.*

BILLY BOB *rushes up to him [enters frame left]. He flashes his badge.*

AMADEUS, *entering frame right, grabs* MEEK's *arm.)*

AMADEUS: You are under arrest.

*(*TATJANA *approaches from upstage.)*

TATJANA: Shut up, that's my line.

BILLY BOB: You may remain silent,

or everything you say may be held against you.

(LIL *runs in, frame left.*)

LIL: Forget it, let's not waste any time . . .

Pull In to Tight Medium on LIL.

LIL *(turns to camera):* We'll have only ten more minutes on this movie . . . Hurry up . . .

Pan with LIL *as she runs out of the frame.*

Cut to MEEK *and* TATJANA. *Medium Shot.*

MEEK: What are you arresting me for?

TATJANA: You are wanted for jewel theft.

Cut to AMADEUS, *Medium.*

AMADEUS: Open your satchel.

Cut to BILLY BOB.

BILLY BOB *(threateningly):* Please.

On MEEK *and* TATJANA.

MEEK: I can't.

TATJANA: Why not?

(MEEK *looks at* TATJANA. *He knows he has been caught. There is no way out. He looks at his satchel.*

CU.

TATJANA, *waiting.*

CU.

BILLY BOB, *waiting.*

CU.

AMADEUS, *waiting.*

Tight Medium on MEEK.

He sighs. He looks at the satchel again.

Tilt Down to CU satchel.

On MEEK'*s hands and the satchel, as he opens the satchel slowly — ever so slowly.*

Tilt Up.

He opens the satchel slightly.

Pull Back to Medium.

On MEEK, *opening the satchel more. He*

turns his head away, he does not dare to look at the jewelry in his satchel. But TATJANA, BILLY BOB, *and* AMADEUS — *all eager anticipation — lean over the satchel.*

CU TATJANA.

Her expression changes, she is puzzled.

CU BILLY BOB.

Furious.

CU AMADEUS.

Amused.

Tight Medium on MEEK.

MEEK *dares to look into the satchel. His eyes widen . . .)*

Medium Shot on MEEK.

MEEK *(smiling):* All right. I give up.

Pull Back to include TATJANA, BILLY BOB, *and* AMADEUS.

MEEK: Go ahead, arrest me.

¾ Shot.

TATJANA: What happened?

BILLY BOB: Crook.

Pan with MEEK *as he leaves.*

MEEK: Have a nice day.

Cut Back to AMADEUS, *Medium.*

*(*AMADEUS *shakes his head, then he sighs admiringly.)*

Pull In on AMADEUS.

AMADEUS: Magician . . .

This particular scene illustrates the following:

- A static group scene works if it has inherent suspense.
- A static group scene requires quick cuts and constant variation of picture size.
- A static group scene demands close attention to *detail*.
- A static scene has to be built on *motive* and *reaction*.

FIGHT SCENE

Fight scenes, like large group scenes, may be shot by using either three cameras or one camera. But regardless of the method you choose, make certain that you'll have a great number of CU bridging shots of faces, fists, guns, knives, etc.

Once the characters participating in a fight have been established, it is a *poor* choice to continue in Full Shots and ¾ Shots while intercutting with a few Medium Shots and CUs. Restrict yourself to about two or three ¾ Shots *at the most*. All other angles have to be CUs and Tight Medium Shots.

To make difficult fight scenes easier to set up and shoot, it is imperative that—regardless of how fast the fight moves—you follow the logical sequence of Motive, Reaction, and Action:

A punches B (motive)
B sees punch coming (reaction)
B punches back (action)

It is always better to shoot a fight scene *without* interruption. Also, shoot a fight scene several times from different angles, remembering that since you will *bridge,* you do not have to concern yourself about the center line. Don't forget that a fight scene *cannot* be edited in the camera but has to be worked on in the editing room. Once you are ready to cut your fight scene, go for *short* takes that move quickly in the sequence of Motive, Reaction, Action.

The following sample fight scene is from *Four Blind Mice* (Ciara Productions, 1992).

Establishing Shot.	**Benji's Bar. Day.**
	(A small, run-down place in East Los Angeles. BENJI, *a huge man, looms behind the bar.* JOE *and* ALEX, *perched on bar stools, nurse their beers.)*
	BENJI: What is it you two guys want?
Pull In to Medium Shot.	ALEX: Actually . . . we are interested in a friend of yours . . . Jeff Biles.
	JOE: He has taken a powder.
	ALEX: Rather suddenly.
	BENJI *(laughs):* So he has flown the coop.

Cut to BENJI. *He is busy stacking some beer glasses.*	BENJI: I never squeal on my friends.
Pull In tighter on BENJI.	BENJI: You two guys better get out before I feel funny.
Low angle on BENJI.	BENJI: Real funny.
Tight Medium on ALEX *and* JOE.	JOE: Take it easy . . .
On BENJI. *Tight Medium. Quickly* BENJI *grabs the detectives' beer glasses.*	(VO) JOE: . . . you are talking to police.
On JOE *and* ALEX, *their POV.*	*(Their distorted view of* BENJI *as the beer hits their faces.*
On BENJI. *He grabs a bottle, smashes it against the bar.*	
CU.	*On the bottle's broken edge.*
Tight Medium on BENJI. *Pan with* BENJI.	*Lifting the bottle, he rushes out from behind the bar.*
Flash: CU.	*Reaction shot* ALEX.
Tight Medium.	JOE *lunging at* BENJI.
Medium.	BENJI *lunging at* JOE.
CU.	*The raised bottle.*
Medium. On JOE *and* BENJI.	JOE *countering the blow.*
CU.	*Edge of bottle hits* JOE's *face.*
Medium JOE, BENJI, ALEX.	ALEX *grabs* BENJI.
	JOE *gets hold of the bottle.*
CU.	JOE *punches bottle out of* BENJI's *hand.*
CU.	*On* BENJI *breathing hard.*
Medium on BENJI, ALEX.	ALEX *slams his fist into* BENJI's *stomach.*
Medium on BENJI.	BENJI *doubles over.*
Medium, BENJI *and* JOE.	JOE *pulls* BENJI's *head back.*

CU BENJI.	BENJI *screams.*
Tight Medium.	JOE *grabs* BENJI *by his throat.*
CU on BENJI.	*Reaction.*
CU on JOE.	*Reaction.*
Medium on BENJI, ALEX, *and* JOE.	*With one quick move* BENJI *gets loose. He grabs* JOE.
Tilt Down.	ALEX *throws* BENJI *on the ground.*
Tight Medium.	BENJI's *fist punches into* ALEX's *face.*
Pull Back.	JOE *jumps on* BENJI's *back.*
Tilt Up.	BENJI *and* JOE *roll on the floor.* JOE *jumps up.*
	ALEX *pulls his gun, points it at* BENJI.)
Cut to BENJI.	*(VO)* ALEX: Sing.
	BENJI: You ain't got the guts to use your gun.
Tight CU on ALEX.	*(Silent, he stares at* BENJI.
Tight CU on BENJI.	BENJI *stares back.*
Tight Medium on ALEX.	*His gun is pointed at* BENJI.
Tight Medium (flash).	JOE.
CU BENJI.	*He looks from* ALEX *to* JOE.
Medium on JOE.	*Silent.*
Medium on ALEX.	*Silent. He lifts the gun.*
CU.	ALEX's *finger moves to the trigger.*
CU.	BENJI *looks at* ALEX.
Tight Medium.	JOE *looks at* ALEX's *hand.*
CU on the gun.	ALEX's *finger moves closer.*
CU on BENJI.	*He hardly dares to breathe.*

CU *on* JOE.	JOE *shakes his head, he looks at* ALEX.
Medium Shot on ALEX.	*Reluctantly* ALEX *puts the gun down.*
Medium on BENJI.	*He lifts his head.)*
Pull Out to include ALEX *and* JOE. BENJI, *hurt all over, gets up.*	BENJI: One of these days I'll get you. You know what they say about police brutality.

Finally, here are a few Dos and Don'ts that will make camera setups and movements a little easier for you. Here we go:

DOs

- If you *begin* a scene with an actor walking into a shot, Pan with the actor. Do *not* have your actor walk into a frame.
- Use Tilts as your actor either gets up or sits down. If you change picture size (¾ to Medium, for instance), do *not* forget to *overlap*.
- Light all CUs carefully. Use backlighting, and if your leading lady is past her first youth, or if she has skin problems, put silks over the lights and position umbrellas close to the lights.
- Pull In and Pull Out gives movement to the beginning of a scene.
- Unless you need an Establishing Shot, considering your film's rental video market, a ¾ Shot is preferable to a Full Shot.
- If you shoot a lengthy dialog scene that for some reason cannot be accommodated by a tracking camera, or if you film a seated dialog scene, acquire movement by having extras move either behind or in front of your actors.
- If possible, move your camera *and* your actors.
- In a seated Two-Shot, have actors *do* something—have them drink a cup of coffee, or let them doodle on a notepad, etc.—but make them *move*.
- Watch screen direction, and use CU bridge shots to change directions.
- In a large group scene, first establish the group in a full shot, then cut to individual groups. Depend on reaction shots, CUs, and Reversals. Every so often cut back to a Full Shot of the group.
- Tight Medium is best for dialog scenes.
- CU is best for reaction shots and short verbal responses. It is less effective for any lengthy dialog.

- *Always* edit in your camera as you write your shooting script.
- Fight scenes and action scenes, however, are the exception. These need to be edited in the editing room. For such scenes use either a three-camera setup or shoot the traditional way (Full Shot, Medium Shot, CU). Don't concern yourself about screen direction but have plenty of CU Bridge Shots. As you edit concentrate on short, quickly moving segments. Once the participants have been established, *avoid* lengthy ¾ or Full Shots, and concentrate on CUs, flash cuts, Tight Medium, and Medium Shots.
- In Reversals watch eye lines and the setup of each actor.
- In a Reversal have the actor *on* camera and the actor *off* camera wait *one beat* (the count of "one thousand and one") before speaking his or her lines. If there is no space between lines, you will have difficulties editing the scene.
- Always *cut* on movement, and *overlap*.

DON'Ts

- Do *not* cut from a Full Shot to a CU. Either Pull In or cut to a Medium Shot and then cut to a CU.
- In a Reversal, picture sizes should be identical. Do not cut from a Medium Shot on actor *A* to a CU on actor *B*.
- Background should not interfere with actors. Do not place your actor in such a way that a picture or vase grows out of his head.
- Avoid placing your actor:
    In the middle of the frame
    Too far to the side
- Changing from location to location, *do not:*
    Begin each scene with a static shot.
    Have an identical picture size ending one scene
        and beginning the next.
- Actors' hand and body movements should not be too fast.
- Don't fail to shoot a sufficient number of CUs for bridge shots.
- Failure to "match" might force you to substitute a bland Full or ¾ Shot for the more interesting combination of Medium Shots and CUs.
- Failure to write a detailed shooting script *will* extend your shooting schedule and *will* make your film more expensive.

4.

The

Fluid Camera

Much of a film's emotional statement depends on camera angles and movements. But keep in mind that none of these should be chosen arbitrarily. Therefore, make certain that you and your camera director are on the same wavelength, that you envision the motion picture going in front of the camera in the same way. Holding detailed talks during the preproduction period, as well as making an effort to understand, consider, and respect each other's point of view, are invaluable.

Confer again and again and again, *before* your film goes on the floor. At times the decision whether to pan or cut is the cause for distressing—and time-consuming—arguments. To arrive at a solution, consider:

· If you wish to put the viewer into the character's shoes, so to speak, I suggest you pan with the actor. In this instance the viewer moves with the character emotionally.

· If you decide that the viewer should be omnipresent, the one who observes but does not participate in the events, then a cut is more logical.

In any event the audience should never become aware of camera angles or movements. If that happens, you have defeated your purpose.

The following scene illustrates the omnipresent viewer's position.

Establishing Shot. Ben's House. Night.*

215 *(A party is in progress. At one end of the pool a bar is set up. At the other end a combo plays, couples are dancing.*

216 *Pull In on* BEN *and* TED. *Holding drinks, they observe the proceedings.)*

TED: I don't think your hobnobbing with the upper crust serves your purpose.

BEN *(shrugs):* I have to. It's business, that's how I make my contacts.

*(*BEN *moves out of the frame. Hold on* TED.

212 TED*'s POV.* BEN *approaches the bar.)*

BEN: Scotch on the rocks.

(On BARTENDER *fixing the drink.*

218 *Cut to* TED *observing* BEN. *Medium Shot.*

219 *Cut to* BEN, *gulping his drink. Medium Shot.*

220 *Cut back to* TED, *observing.* MARGE *[*BEN*'s wife] enters the frame. Pull Back.)*

MARGE *(slightly drunk):* Hey Ted ... good to see you, haven't been around for a while.

(She looks around.)

MARGE: Take a look at all this glitz, look at all those diamonds ... Well, excuse me, I'll have to keep circulating ...

(Pan with her as she joins BEN *at the bar.)*

MARGE: I ... I ... feel like poor Cinderella ...

BEN: Spare me your comments ... please.

221 *(Medium on* MARGE, *feeling sorry for herself. Gesturing to the dancing couples, she mumbles.)*

Four Blind Mice (Ciara Productions, 1992).

MARGE: This crowd is poison for us.

222 *(Cut to* TED, *smiling to himself.)*

And now a different scene, where the fluid camera establishes the character's apprehension, and puts the viewer into her shoes.

Abandoned Tenement. Staircase. Night.

456 *(Long Shot. Camera framing through the banister.* AHNA *enters shot. Her flashlight casts eerie shadows.*
Pull In to ¾ Shot as AHNA *walks up the stairs. Pan with her.*
Hold on AHNA. *Her flashlight explores the wall.*

457 AHNA's *POV. The wall. Paint peels off. Graffiti covers the wall.*

458 *Back on* AHNA. *Pull Back as* AHNA *ascends the stairs and Pan. Pan with* AHNA *as she enters the hallway. Again she stops, looks around. Tight Medium Shot.*

459 AHNA's *POV. A door leading to one of the apartments.*

460 *Back on* AHNA, *Pan with her as she approaches the door.*
Over the shoulder, AHNA. *We notice that the door stands slightly ajar. Pull In to Tight Medium.*

462 AHNA's *POV. Shock Zoom: the door is thrown open and a shadow looms over her.)*

Editing for Logic

When we speak about the fluid camera, we also have to concern ourselves with editing. It is editing that pulls all the bits and pieces of angles and camera movements into a logical unit. The beginning director does not have the luxury of shooting every scene from various angles, and consequently has to decide on editing methods *before* the first shooting day. The beginning director has to decide on the editing method to be employed while *writing* the shooting script. There are four basic types of editing:

Subjective editing
Point-of-view editing

Invisible editing
Empathic editing

Keep in mind, both camera work and editing have to further the dramatic purpose of your film.

SUBJECTIVE EDITING

Depending on the power of the CU, subjective editing lets the viewer observe events through the character's eyes. Most likely you will use subjective editing if you want your audience to expect something to happen.

276 **Urban Street. Day.**
   (Establishing Shot of a dilapidated urban street bordered by a row of run-down tenements. BOB's car stops in front of one of the buildings.)
277 **Interior Bob's Car. Day.**
   (Medium Shot on BOB. Leaning out of the car window, he looks up at the tenement.
278 *CU on the tenement looming in front of him [Tilt Shot].*
279 *Back on BOB, Medium Shot. He hesitates for a beat, then reaches for his gun.*
280 *CU. BOB's POV, the gun.)*

   Urban Street. Day.
281 *(Pull Back to ¾ Shot. BOB gets out of the car; Pan with him as he approaches the tenement.)*
   Interior Tenement. Hallway.
282 *(BOB, pointing his gun, enters. He stops, looks around.)*

This is subjective editing—the audience has been put into a character's shoes.

POINT-OF-VIEW EDITING

Point-of-view editing stresses the *facts* in a scene. It does not attempt to interpret the characters' reaction to a given situation; neither does it put the viewer into the characters' shoes. The viewer remains omnipresent, knows everything, sees everything, and remains emotionally uninvolved.

Now let's take a look at the previous scene employing point-of-view editing.

276 **Urban Street. Day.**
(Establishing Shot of a dilapidated urban street bordered by a row of run-down tenements. BOB's car stops in front of one of the buildings.
Pull In as BOB gets out of the car. Pan with him as he walks toward the tenement.)

As you can tell, since the CUs (Bob's POV) have been omitted, we *see* Bob's action, but we have no clue as to his *reaction* to the event.

INVISIBLE EDITING

Invisible editing is keyed to *movements*. Each take begins with movement and ends with movement. Invisible editing is important for scenes that are static by nature, as it keeps such scenes moving.

276 **Urban Street. Day.**
(Full Shot on BOB's car driving.)
277 **Interior Bob's Car. Day.**
(On BOB driving.
He reaches for his gun.
278 *CU his hand on the gun.*
279 *Back on BOB, driving. He lifts the gun.)*
280 **Exterior Urban Street. Day.**
(BOB's car stops.
281 *Different angle. ¾ Shot, BOB gets out of the car.)*
282 **Tenement Interior. Hallway. Day.**
(On TED, walking to the door. He stops. Pulls out a knife.)
283 **Urban Street. Day.**
(On BOB, walking to the tenement's front door. Pan with him, his hand reaches for the door handle.)
284 **Interior Tenement. Day.**
(On TED. Slowly he lifts his knife.)
285 **Exterior Tenement. Day.**
(BOB kicks the door open.)

In this example, the audience is in the omnipresent position. Looking at the scene location directions, you will notice that the entire scene has been based on the actors' movements.

EMPATHIC EDITING

Empathic editing relies on the contrast of rhythm and *visual pattern*. This method, pioneered by famous silent movie director D. W. Griffith, uses *crosscutting* (interweaving bits of two or more scenes), *pacing,* and *emotional juxtaposition.* Here is an example:

Ted's House. Pool Area. Day.

275 *(¾ Shot on dancing couples.*

276 *Different angle on dancing couples. Pull In on a dancing couple, Pan to* BEN *watching the dancing, Pull In on* BEN *to Tight Medium. He lifts his champagne glass and takes a sip.)*

277 **Exterior Urban Street. Day.**
    (On car driving, headlights move — CU — to camera.)

278 **Interior Tenement. Hallway.**
    (CU feet descending stairs. Tilt Up to Tight Medium on TED *and hold.)*

279 **Interior Ted's House. Pool Area. Day.**
    (On dancing couples reflected in pool.

280 *Various angles on dancing couples.*

281 *Various angles on dancing couples.*

282 *Various angles on dancing couples.)*

283 **Exterior Tenement. Day.**
    (¾ Shot, BOB *gets out of his car. Pan with him as he walks toward the tenement. Hold as he stops in front of the door.)*

284 **Interior Tenement. Hallway. Day.**
    (Medium Shot on TED, *standing and waiting.)*

285 **Exterior Tenement. Night.**
    (On BOB. *He pulls out his gun.*

286 *On gun.*

287 *Flash cuts: Tight Medium on dancing couples*
    BEN *waiting*
    CU gun
    TED *waiting*

> *Dancing couples*
> *CU gun*
> 288 *Tight Medium,* BOB *lifts his gun.)*
> 289 **Interior Tenement. Hallway. Day.**
> *(On* TED. *He lifts his knife.)*

In this example of empathic editing, the audience is in the omnipresent position.

The sample scenes show clearly the importance of deciding on editing methods *before* going in front of the camera; they show how the same basic scene, depending on the manner of editing, can have an entirely different scenic logic. My advice is that you choose your editing methods while writing the shooting script.

It is true, the director with a substantial budget can shoot more extensive coverage by filming a scene from various angles. This allows the luxury of deciding on editing methods during the editing process. But I seriously doubt that such creative freedom will actually make for a better film. To have an extensive amount of material at one's disposal raises the danger of placing more emphasis on creative editing than on the film's narrative. I feel it is easier (and far less expensive) to check a film's pace, logical flow, emotional content, and narrative clarity via a detailed shooting script than via your Moviola. (Using a Moviola will be further discussed in chapter 7.)

Pacing

Take a good look at the previous scene, and you'll know that pacing is the inherent *rhythm* of a scene. This rhythm might be visual (seascape *vs.* hectic downtown traffic) or emotional (lonely old woman *vs.* children at a birthday party); it might be inherent in the sound accompanying a scene or in your actors' dialog. However it is achieved, pacing indicates the rate of movement, progress, and/or emotional juxtaposition. If you are working with a sufficiently structured script, and if you have worked out a detailed shooting script, chances are you needn't worry. If, however, you came up with some "creative" ideas during shooting, you may be well advised to look closely at pacing and at the logical development of your film.

It is also possible that the middle of your film, regardless of a tightly written shooting script, drags here and there. The fault might be that the scenes are pictorially too *uniform* (too many Medium Shots). If this is the case, look through your cover shots and insert a *logical* CU here and there. On the other hand, some scenes, even though well varied pictorially, seem to be static. This often happens in a scene based on a verbal confrontation. Unfortunately once the film is in the editing room, there is little you can do about it. Even inserting CUs won't help the visual flow. Maybe, just maybe, you will be able to add some variation by employing background sounds. (We will discuss sound in the concluding portion of this chapter.) If sound doesn't help, all you can do—short of reshooting, which I advise against—is admit that you have made a mistake, have learned a valuable lesson, and will remember to use Pan and Track Shots wherever logically appropriate.

If a scene seems to go on forever, check the dialog for:

Repetitions
Irrelevancies
Long, involved sentences

Needless to say, all these flaws should have been corrected in writing the shooting script, but if a "guppy" does slip through now and then, you should have no difficulty editing out the bothersome little mistake if you have had the foresight to shoot plenty of reaction and environmental ambience shots:

- If you are unable to edit repetitions and irrelevancies, show a reaction shot of a character reacting to them and VO the other character's dialog.
- If you are unable to edit out segments of long, involved sentences, show environmental ambience shots and VO dialog.

Here is an example:

The Van Burens' Living Room. Day.

134 (MRS. VAN BUREN *explains to* BUFFY, *her daughter, why she should marry elderly Richard Galen.*)

MRS. VAN BUREN: Buffy, my angel, you know that I had always—and have now—only your best at heart. Your future has been on my mind . . .

135 *(On BUFFY, sitting erect, sipping tea demurely. Smiling bitterly, she keeps herself from erupting with anger.)*

(VO) MRS. VAN BUREN: . . . husband, your dear father, had the audacity to leave his wife, and you, his daughter, to find happiness with a manicurist . . .

136 *(CU of desk with family pictures.)*

(VO) MRS. VAN BUREN: . . . a circus trapeze artist . . .

137 *(Cut to Mr. Van Buren's stern-looking oil portrait hanging over the mantel).*

(VO) MRS. VAN BUREN: . . . and last, but not least, I suppose . . . with the lady taxidermist. Darling Richard Galen would never . . .

138 *(Cut to stuffed moose head on the wall.)*

(VO) MRS. VAN BUREN: . . . ever show such inconsistency.

(Back on MRS. VAN BUREN.)

MRS. VAN BUREN: He is the man you should entrust your future to.

Strange as it may seem, even the most exciting car chase, shoot-out, or fight scene becomes tiresome if dragged out too long. I know such scenes are expensive to shoot, and no director wants to see one foot of precious film land on the cutting floor. But contain yourself; realize that the audience's attention span is much shorter than the director's. If, however, a relatively short car chase or fight scene seems too long, you can bet your last production dollar that this particular scene lacks *detail*. All action scenes must *involve* the viewer, and it is detail that does the trick. For an example, turn back to the fight scene shooting script in the previous chapter under "Difficult Setups Made a Little Easier" and look at all the detail shown in this scene.

Probably the least obvious, and therefore often overlooked, reason for drag is that the director has disregarded *time expansion* and *time compression*.

These two qualities are most likely to be forgotten in the script rewrite, and are easily overlooked in the shooting script.

TIME EXPANSION

Let's say your script states: "Adam aims and fires. Frank, hit, topples back and falls off the roof." That sounds simple, but believe me, you are faced with a difficult shot. Remember, you want your audience to cheer brave Adam, but you also want them to participate in the shock of Frank's fall. You want to make this scene exciting.

So you have rented an expensive western town location, obtained huge air bags to soften Frank's fall, have set up three cameras, and paid a sizable stuntman's fee. You are all set to get your money's worth. On the screen, unfortunately, the fall is less than impressive. It looks something like this:

101 *(Full Shot of* ADAM *hitting* FRANK. FRANK, *clutching his chest, begins to topple.*
102 FRANK *falling.*
103 *Full Shot as the townspeople gather around* FRANK's *body.)*

You are at a loss and ask yourself why the fall didn't work. The answer will be found in the fact that the fall seen on the screen took exactly as long as it took the stuntman to fall. Time expansion—stringing visual detail on visual detail—encompasses more time than it takes for the fall to be completed, and therefore makes the fall visually impressive.

Now take another look at Frank's fall:

101 *(¾ Shot. Tilt Up to* FRANK *as he clutches his chest.*
102 *On* ADAM *watching.*
103 *Medium.* FRANK *topples backward.*
104 FRANK's *POV, the townspeople looking up to him. [Camera angle from roof down.]*
105 *Medium shot [against the sky].* FRANK *begins to fall over the edge of the roof.*
106 FRANK's *POV: camera Tilt Down to the side of the building, CU.*
107 *Tilt Up:* FRANK *falls, Medium Shot.*
108 *On townspeople, Medium.*

109 *Other angle on* FRANK *falling,* ¾ *Shot.*
110 *Medium on townspeople, a girl screams.*
111 *Other angle on* FRANK *falling, Tight Medium.*
112 *CU* FRANK *screams.*
113 *Camera on rooftop down, Medium Shot on* FRANK *falling.*
114 *Full Shot, the townspeople gather around* FRANK. *[You cannot show your stuntman landing on the air bag.]*
115 ¾ *Shot, townspeople's POV,* FRANK *lying on the ground.)*

This scene has visual logic:

• Several successively closer shots make the action become larger and larger on the screen.
• The insertion (crosscutting) of the townspeople's reactions, the Tilt Up to the sky, and the Tilt Down to the wall, make the viewer participate in Frank's fall.

Remember the importance of overlapping (matching) for this and any other action scene, and cover yourself by shooting plenty of reaction shots to have on hand to bridge the action.

TIME COMPRESSION

Time compression comes in handy if unnecessary screen time has to be omitted, or if an important part of a segment is missing. Your script calls for Becky to get out of her car, walk up to her parents' house, and enter. The scene looked fine when you shot it, but looking at Becky's walk once you are in the editing room, you know it is too long. You will edit this way:

(Full Shot, BECKY *gets out of her car.*
Cut to Medium Shot, BECKY *rings the doorbell.)*

You will use the same method if for some reason Becky's walk from the car to her parents' house is fine timewise, but has been marred by a technical flaw. If (this happens rarely) you are unable to cut from Becky's car to her parents' door, then use an insert of Becky's mother watching from the window. True, reshooting should usually be avoided. If, however, you need a few inserts or reaction shots (easily done in Tight Medium or CU against a neutral background), then adding a few hours of pickups won't break your budget.

Here is another time compression sequence, which will be effective for a comedy:

408 *(On* HERCULES, *a diminutive man, carrying a huge suitcase. He stops for a moment, looks at his watch, then increases his pace.*

409 *Tight Medium on* HERCULES's *feet running. The suitcase bounces up and down.*

410 *Flash cuts:*   *plane*
                    train
                    bus
                    feet pedaling bicycle

411 *CU on suitcase, Pull Out and Tilt Up, on* HERCULES *standing, waiting. It is hot. He takes out a handkerchief and wipes his face. He looks at his watch.*

412 *CU watch.*

413 *On* HERCULES, *covered with snow.)*

Lighting

A properly (not necessarily artistically) lit scene needs three components:

1. *Key lights* (main light source)
2. *Fill lights* to balance the shadows created by the key lights.
3. *Back lights* to make the actors stand out from the background and give actresses a softer and more beautiful facial appearance.

Excessive Lighting   Often there is the tendency to overlight a film. True, one has to take into consideration that sooner or later the film will play the home video screen. Since the TV screen does not handle shadows well, it is understandable that director and camera director alike shot with one eye (if not both) focused on the requirements of home video distribution. Yet it is the *balance* between light and shadow that creates mood, not the dimness or brightness of the entire picture.

Light Plot   The placement of lights is the camera director's responsibility, using artistic knowledge to convey mood on the screen.

Backlighting   As you and the producer peruse the many demo tapes camera directors will send in, keep your eyes open; make certain that the prospective camera directors know how to create pictures with lights. Also, they should be familiar with the fact that a man needs to be lit different from a woman. Regardless of her age, a woman should—as mentioned previously—be back-lit; that is, the background should be lighter than the actress. The very best light setup for a CU uses a diffused light source from above (about 45 degrees to the camera) and a bright *kicker* light from the side of the camera. Furthermore, make certain to use a scrim* in front of the kicker, an added light source, when photographing a woman.

A scrim   When filming in natural sunlight a scrim is also useful. Natural sunlight needs either to be diffused by a scrim, or augmented by artificial light. Sunlight, keep in mind, is not easy to handle. Improperly handled sunlight will make a beautiful woman look haggard. The same goes for reflected light from a swimming pool or any other light source.

If possible, *avoid* panning from sunlight into the artificial light of a cabin, for example. Such a shot demands an intricate and time-consuming light setup. It is much better to show your actor opening the door in an exterior shot, then closing it in an interior shot.

Rim Lighting   Directors and camera directors alike agree that the very best light source comes from above. I hope you remember the disadvantages of scaffold lighting discussed in chapter 2, and will insist on having lights placed on high stands. If your camera director wants scaffold lighting for dark scenes in a dimly lit place or even quasidarkness, don't give in; suggest rim lighting instead. If set against a dark background, rim lighting (the actor is lit from right and left) leaves an actor's face in shadows. If your actor is supposed to look for something, give him a flashlight to handle, then light the spot where the beam of the flashlight hits. This method needs close coordination between actor and gaffer, as the flashlight and the light have to hit a prop or a person *simultaneously.*

*A length of sheer silk placed in front of a light source.

Likewise, don't ever use scaffolding when filming a hallway scene, or you will remain on your hallway location forever and three days. When lighting a hallway, simply place a light source behind each door leading to the hallway. Keep the doors ajar and you have plenty of light.

If you wish to emphasize some details on a mantel or a door, place light sources at the foot of the architectural detail to beam along the edges of it.

Basic and Secondary Light Plots   As I have mentioned a number of times, changing your lighting plot is time consuming and, therefore, expensive. You will save precious production hours by establishing a basic light plot and a secondary light plot. The basic light plot illuminates the entire area where action takes place; the secondary light plot, necessitating the move of only a few lights, is used to light specific areas as needed. To simplify matters use 500-watt photo floods for these quick light plot changes. Yet the art of lighting encompasses more than lighting actors sufficiently and attractively. Lighting creates space and moods. The right lighting makes a room cheerful or, if you so desire, dismal; it makes an area seem large or claustrophobic; it can trap your characters in shadow or pave their road with gold. It all depends how lights are set up.

Using Locations

At best motion pictures reflect life experiences and show the filmmaker's conclusions about these experiences. Such experiences move either in the realm of the abstract, where the trappings of everyday life turn into metaphors, or they become the background that underscores the reality seen on the screen. In both cases, you the director will have to decide on two basic conceptions:

- Character is in conflict with environment.
- Character is in harmony with environment.

Environmental conflict should never be expressed in dialog ("To look at skyscrapers makes me so dizzy I could scream") but should be expressed *visually.* Only then will the audience have empathy with what is going on in the character's mind. With a little imagination, you won't have difficulties finding appropriate visual metaphors. Two examples follow.

CHARACTER IN CONFLICT WITH ENVIRONMENT

(MARK *has been looking for a job, unsuccessfully. By now he has given up all hope of ever working again, and he is close to a nervous breakdown.*)

Interior Office Building. Hallway. Day.

312 *(Extreme Long Shot on* MARK *walking down the hallway.*

313 MARK's *POV, hand-held camera: the hallway begins to sway,* ¾ *Shot.*

314 *On* MARK, *looking up. Medium Shot.*

315 MARK's *POV. On door, camera Tilt: the door begins to sway.* ¾ *Shot. Quick Tilt Down: the door shuts.* ¾ *Shot.*

316 *Hand-held camera, Medium Shot,* MARK *running down the hallway.*

317 *Track Shot, hand-held camera, frontal on* MARK.

318 MARK's *POV, hand-held camera, Tracking Shot, on the doors, insanely swinging to and fro.*

319 *CU on* MARK.

320 MARK's *POV: In rapid succession, one after the other, the doors close. Hand-held camera, quick Tracking Shot. Crashing sound as each door closes.*

320 *On* MARK, *Medium. High, piercing sound. He stands for a beat, then runs again.*

321 *CU on* MARK's *feet running, piercing sound increases.*

322 *Tight Medium on doors closing, crashing sound. Pull In on last door— explosionlike sound, then silence.)*

Exterior Office Building. Day.

323 *([Please note the time compression from 322 to 323. We do not see* MARK *exiting the building.]* MARK, *exhausted, leans against the front door. The silence continues for a beat, then the piercing sound begins again.* MARK *looks up, the piercing sound increases.*

324 MARK's *POV, extreme Long Shot, on a high-rise building insanely swinging to and fro. Slow Tilt as the building, threatening to crush him, leans toward* MARK.

325 *On* MARK. *Fast Tilt, up to CU.)*

CHARACTER IN HARMONY WITH ENVIRONMENT

(Today is a little girl's first day of vacation.
104 *Extreme Long Shot on* AMY *dancing in a meadow. The telephoto lens, creating a hazy background, gives an impressionistic effect.*
Pull In to a ¾ Shot on AMY. *She continues to dance, as she slowly elevates and begins to float. [We will discuss the special effect of floating in chapter 9.]*
105 AMY's *POV. Extreme Long Shot on the blue, cloud-laced sky.*
106 *Back on* AMY *floating.)*
107 **Exterior Amy's House. Day.**
(On AMY, *her parents, and her dog* POOCHY, *happily loading camping gear into the family car.)*

Visual metaphors are far stronger than any verbally expressed emotion or opinion. This holds especially true as you show your characters within the *reality* of an environment. Here, you and your art director will have to work diligently to make the depicted reality conform to the reality of the characters on the screen.

Take a kitchen, for instance. Every prop—furniture, appliances, kitchen gadgets, even the calendar on the wall—has to conform to the place, time period, and socioeconomic status you wish to portray. A farm kitchen of the 1880s was different from a farm kitchen of today. And a farm kitchen in Iowa is different from a condo kitchen in, say, Los Angeles or Chicago. But a condo kitchen for a young family has a different feel from the one of a single career woman. The gadgets seen in the kitchen of a middle-class suburban home are a far cry from the ones cluttering the kitchenette of a downtown welfare hotel.

Besides furniture and props, you should take walls and window treatments into consideration. Peeling paint *vs.* bright wallpaper, subdued patterns *vs.* flashy ones, a tidy room *vs.* a disorderly one, antique furnishings *vs.* Danish modern: all are silent signals that give powerful clues about the characters occupying a specific location. Since the information given is never verbally stated, the audience will absorb it by osmosis, which is a highly effective way of dispensing information.

Use the look of your location to make an emotional statement about the characters in your film:

• A once-grand mansion, now stripped of all possessions and furnished with only the barest necessities, makes a strong statement about your leading character Lillian's financial and (probably) emotional state.

• A bedroom lovingly decorated with a chintz bedspread and matching draperies, Currier & Ives prints, and country furniture—but also cluttered with overflowing ashtrays, boots, and nail-studded leather outfits—makes a strong statement about Frances as she lolls, smoking a cigarette, on her unmade bed.

• Greg's living room, with its stacks of neatly arranged scientific magazines, extensive computer system, and graphics adorning the wall, tells the viewer immediately that his friendship with Jennifer—a free spirit—will encounter some difficulties.

You, the beginning director, rarely have the luxury of shooting in a pristine studio environment; you'll have to rent actual locations. Seldom do these locations come even close to what you need. Work hard with your art director to create your envisioned environment as nearly as possible.

Production design is one of the most powerful aspects of your film. I cannot stress enough the importance of discussing every detail with your art director. Consider a variety of design approaches, play around with them, try them out, so to speak, on the characters occupying specific locations; after all, it is the preproduction period that gives you the chance to discover and create. Don't ever give in to the temptation of disregarding the importance of environment. You may rationalize, "The actors are terrific, the script is well written, the producer has hired a skilled and creative camera director, so even if my locations are kind of humdrum, the statement I wish to make and the mood I wish to create will come through"—don't fool yourself. The audience will not pick up on mood or statement unless the environment (location) gives them the proper visual clues.

Using Sound

Sound, like locations, is an integral and very important part of your movie. We classify sounds into:

Dialog
Natural sound and sound effects
Music

Don't try to save on either sound equipment or operator. Your sound equipment must be of excellent quality (I recommend the Nagra system and Sennheiser directional microphones), and your operator has to be highly skilled, if you want clear-sounding sync dialog.

RECORDING DIALOG

Microphone placement is important. A closely placed microphone minimizes any background noises (important for exterior locations) and gives "pressure" to the actor's voice—that is, the actor's voice seems close to the audience.

Sync Sound   A Nagra recorder is equipped with an oscillator identical to the sync pulse generator that controls the camera speed. In this way sound and picture are shot synchronously, or in movie terms, *sync*. During the editing process each of the camera takes is lined up sync with its corresponding sound track.

When using sync sound for dialogue, always use a *noiseless* camera. Unfortunately no camera is completely noiseless. Besides *blimping* (putting a cover over your camera), you may employ a telephoto lens and place the camera at a distance from your actors.

And then, of course, you can always hide some unwanted noise with natural sound and sound effects.

NATURAL SOUND AND SOUND EFFECTS

Sound reveals and strengthens the reality of the moment. We see the plane taking off as we hear the roar of the engines; we see the door of the abandoned house open as we hear the screech of the unoiled hinges. In other words, a distinctive sound is particular to a distinct action. Sound continuously supplies your audience with information. Even sound without action can turn into a source of information, and at times is more expressive than the combination of action and sound. This is a blessing for the beginning director, who should consider substituting sound for an action shot or special effect. For instance, the audience does not have to see Bobby throwing a football through the plate glass window. It is equally effective to hear the shattering of glass while we see Bobby's reaction.

Natural sound is an effective device to express a location's atmosphere and a scene's mood. Bells tolling, a faucet dripping, add considerably to a scene's anguish, while a fire crackling in a fireplace and the soft sound of rain on trees set a tranquil mood.

The *distortion* of sound and voices helps to express a character's emotion in a symbolic way (as we saw in the example illustrating character in conflict with environment). Amplification is an excellent device to make a sound even more disturbing. A finger stabbing on a wooden surface, voices attacking from all directions, a telephone ringing incessantly — amplified, these make a powerful statement.

Natural sound is also effective if used as *counterpoint* — that is, in contrast to the visual image on the screen. For instance, on the screen we see an old, frail lady lovingly placing a doll in a box, while we hear the happy squeals of a children's birthday party and the song "Happy Birthday to You."

Within the confines of a scene, natural sound should match from take to take (or angle to angle). Granted, this is sometimes impossible to achieve. For this reason you should *always* make it a habit to record some natural sound (ambience, also called room sound), to add where needed during the editing process.

MUSIC

Either composed especially for your film, or canned (prerecorded), music pulls your film together. Even though the audience is unaware of it, background music does add considerably to the visual power of the pictures seen on the screen. Background music:

- Conveys information.
- Serves to establish continuity as it carries over from one scene to the next, or from one location to the next.
- Serves to establish the mood of a scene or location.
- Expresses the *actor's* emotion.

At times background music is used in a less than effective way, especially if it provides just any sound, instead of giving *specific* information about a place or a situation. After all, we do expect to hear a string quartet playing some old-fashioned tunes as we view the exterior of an elegant turn-of-the-century hotel, not some insignificant elevator music.

Even worse, music can give false information. Take, for instance, Little Red Riding Hood, happily skipping through the forest on her way to Grandmother's house. Yes, *we* know that the Big Bad Wolf is hiding behind the trees. But does Little Red know? Of course not. So, if we hear ominous music accompanying her scampering, *we* the audience (who ought to be in Little Red's shoes) are misled. The music *must always match* the character's emotion. The tune we hear should be happy and lighthearted, but *change* the moment the Big Bad Wolf reveals himself.

Continuing music as well as continuing sound should be used to carry the audience from one scene to the next. Imagine, if you will, a scene taking place at a carnival. We cut from the merry-go-round to the children crowding around a booth that sells cotton candy, to a barker announcing his nerve-shattering attractions, to the glittering wheel of fortune, all pulled together by snatches of music, voices, and laughter. Now all these sounds will continue, diminished of course, as we cut to the tender scene of Sally and Tim kissing in back of the magician's trailer.

Part Three

5.

The Director

and

Actors

You, the director, know that actors make or break your film. Once you have selected an exciting script, labored over your shooting script, found perfect locations, and — in concert with the producer — hired a skilled camera director, you need actors to make your vision come alive. The right actors, who look the part and act the part, as the old saying goes, will make your motion picture sparkle, while mediocre ones may make your picture mundane. Agreed, a poorly written script cannot be revived by excellent acting, while a solid script cannot be ruined by uninspired acting (after all, many a crafty editor has turned a questionable performance into an acceptable one), but such motion pictures lack vitality and consequently fail to grip the audience.

So, how do you go about finding these scintillating actors who, through their skill and personality, succeed in drawing the viewer into the world on the screen?

Let's admit it: the kind of actor you need is not necessarily brilliant and/ or good looking, but is the one who has a solid acting background, is skilled in on-camera acting techniques, and, most important, has screen personality, or charisma.

Now, what is screen personality? It is not a God-given, intangible, and therefore exciting talent; stated very simply, it is an actor's ability to communicate with the audience by expressing believable emotions that in turn arouse the viewers' emotions.

Believable emotions are simple. They are expressed in a straightforward manner. Believable emotions never try to impress an audience with the depth of the actor's feelings or the brilliance of the acting technique displayed. The actor makes the audience see a *person,* not an actor playing a part. And this brings us to the subject of communication.

The actor who has screen personality connects with the audience in a subtle way. It is the actor-audience communication that draws the viewer into the events on the screen, and not, as many producers contend, million-dollar production values such as special effects, car chases, and exotic locations. The actor communicates with the viewer in two ways that are continuously interchangeable:

- The viewer becomes the character's partner.
- By the process of osmosis the viewer feels addressed, threatened, or embraced by the character on the screen.
- The viewer becomes the character on the screen and participates in his or her adventures.

In short, the most effective motion picture acting permits the viewer to participate in the events on the screen. You should assemble your cast with utmost attention to the visual power of every one of your actors. Think about your cast as a tapestry whose colors (your actors) have to complement one another, contrast effectively, yet blend harmoniously. In other words, their looks and demeanor should contrast sufficiently to make each *character* stand out in his or her own right, yet blend in with the rest of the cast.

This is the moment when the threatening concept of typecasting rears its ugly head. Agreed, a hood is supposed to look like a hood, a nun like a nun, a college professor like a college professor, and a socialite like a socialite, but do not present your audience with types they have seen over and over ad nauseam. Types that one recognizes immediately tend to become boring. Only types that, while recognizable, still manage to challenge the audience will add the necessary spice to your film. For this reason never insist that a character has to have a certain look; in the search for just the right type you may overlook another and better actor. For my motion picture *Frozen Scream*

I was looking for an Irish priest. I had found the ideal type, but instead I cast an Italian-looking actor for the role. Why? Simple: the second actor had screen personality, whereas the first one had only the look.

The Casting Process

In case you have to contend with a rather bland "star" (an actor whose name value your distributor insists upon), you ought to surround your star with effective and impressive actors. And this brings us to casting your picture. Most likely the distributor—if you are in the fortunate position of working for a producer who has a distribution contract—will suggest a few recognizable names, and it is the producer's responsibility to contact the respective actors. First the producer will contact the actor's agency to find out about the star's availability. The producer will negotiate with the agent; you as director are more or less out of the picture. The same holds true for the rest of the cast.

A production company that is able to attract a recognizable star will most definitely hire a casting director. The casting director lists the roles to be cast with the Breakdown Service, and the agents in turn submit their clients' names. For each part to be cast the casting director will present you with three or four choices. You, at times in concert with the producer, will have the final decision. Here a word of warning: the casting director might not supply you with the most exciting or talented actors. He or she will, however, bring in actors who have experience—that is to say, actors who are on time, have learned their lines, and know how to hit a mark.

USING UNION ACTORS

Admittedly SAG (Screen Actors Guild) actors are not necessarily better trained or more talented than nonunion actors. Let me explain: unless an actor has been hired by either a TV show, feature film, or commercial production company that is signatory with SAG, he or she cannot join the Screen Actors Guild.

There are many members of SAG who are not trained actors but were able to join via a TV commercial. Conversely, there are many—yes, thousands—of well-trained and highly talented actors who never had the opportunity to work for a commercial, TV show, or feature film shot by a production company signatory with SAG, and for this reason they are ineligible to join SAG. Many of these actors join AFTRA (American Federation of Radio and Television Artists). This union, covering radio and live TV (soaps, some game shows, and situation comedies), does not require—as SAG does—*proof of work*. Anyone, actor or nonactor, is permitted to join. Once a member of AFTRA works as a *principal* (a role with more than five speaking lines), he or she is eligible to join SAG, one year after the date the AFTRA contract was signed. An actor who worked as an extra (nonspeaking) for an AFTRA show is not eligible to join SAG.

Things look quite different if you are working on a low-budget feature where you, in concert with the producer, are faced with the entire casting process from A to Z.

Let's assume the production company that hired you is signatory with SAG, and adheres to the union's rules and regulations. This means you will be able to cast *SAG actors only,* and are prohibited from hiring a mix of union and nonunion actors. You have, of course, the opportunity to have a non-SAG actor admitted to SAG via your feature film. All your producer has to do is write a letter to SAG, requesting that the actor be admitted to the union. Again, your roster of roles to be cast will be listed with the Breakdown Service, and agents will submit their clients.

And now let's speak about the situation you will find yourself in if you work for a production company that has not signed with SAG. Obviously no agency will submit any of their clients to a nonsignatory company. You and, most likely, the producer are responsible for the entire casting process. Since the Breakdown Service will not accept your casting list, you should send your casting requirements to *Hollywood Drama-logue* and *Casting Call* if you live in Los Angeles, and *Back Stage* if you live close to New York. In places not featuring *trades* (trade magazines), you might get in contact with your local college's cinema or telecommunication department or drama department and ask for permission to post a casting notice on the bulletin board. If you do not have access to a college, pursue your local community theater and any drama schools that teach acting for the camera.

Have your financing all arranged before you start casting. Sending out casting notices before you are positive that your project will go in front of the camera is unfair to you and the actors involved. But take your time casting. Do not rush. About three months prior to your shooting date, when you are in preproduction, is a good time to begin your casting process.

HEADSHOTS AND RESUMES

My advice is to look at the actors' submitted headshots (8 × 10 photos) *before* you read resumes. An impressive resume might easily lead you to consider an actor who has extensive credits but turns out to be wrong as far as age and type are concerned. (This, I admit, should not keep you from casting "against type" if you find an outstanding actor.) It is a good idea to sort submissions into groups:

Suitable age and type
Unsuitable age and type, but interesting
Hopeless

Refrain from making any decision as yet. Do not call in actors for auditions, but permit your creative forces to simmer a little before you go through the photos again. At this point pay special attention to your "unsuitable but interesting" file; you may find just the right actor in this particular group. True, the actor might not be exactly the right type for the part you have in mind, but there might be something special about him or her. If you have a gut feeling about an actor go with it, and call the actor in for a reading.

As soon as you have identified several possible actors for each part, it is time to take a good look at resumes. But here a word of warning: the most impressive resume might not indicate the most qualified actor; in other words, the resume might not reflect the actor's true qualifications. I am not speaking about a fictitious resume — in twelve years of producing I have rarely come upon one. Actors are honest people, but at times they are prone to *glorify* the work they have done. The beginning director may rather easily fall into their innocently set traps.

Take actress *A*, for instance. She lists a number of recent box office hits, but since she doesn't list SAG membership, you know she worked as an extra (providing atmosphere) on these movies. Extra work, unfortunately, does not give you any information about her acting ability. It is true that many excellent actors, in order to make a living, *do* extra work, but they refrain from listing it on a resume. If you see extra work listed, you know you are dealing with an actor of limited experience.

Actor *B* lists a number of stage credits, but mentions no theater where the plays were performed. There is no doubt that *B* performed these roles in acting class, not onstage.

Actor *C* has a solid stage background but lacks film credits. Since he has not attended an on-camera class, it is unlikely that C will perform adequately in front of your camera.

Actress D's resume, at first glance, does not look impressive. But she has attended on-camera classes as well as a number of acting courses conducted by respected coaches. Actress D has participated in a number of student films (she mentions that a demo tape is available), and gained stage experience via college and community theaters. Here you're faced with an actress who has prepared herself quite well. At least you know D is familiar with basic acting techniques, is able to hit marks, and knows how to perform in front of a camera. Confidently you may call in actress D.

An actor's resume should list:

- *Actor's name* and (if not represented by an agency) telephone number.
- *Union affiliation* (SAG, AFTRA).
- *Film and TV credits.* The actor should list such credits *only* if he or she had speaking lines, regardless of whether the film mentioned was a SAG production, nonunion film, or student production.
- *Stage credits.* All stage credits for legitimate theater, college, and community theater should be given.
- *Workshops.* This segment of an actor's resume is important for you, the director, as it tells that the actor, by attending workshops, keeps his or her skills sharpened.
- *Training.* Another important segment that shows how well the actors have prepared themselves for their chosen profession.
- *Sports.* Needless to say, this segment lists the sports an actor can do.
- *Special abilities.* If the actor is an accomplished athlete, singer, dancer, etc., it will be mentioned here.

INTERVIEWS

I would recommend that you *not* lock yourself into a mental image of how a character in your film should look and act. Keep an open mind as you interview your actors. Maybe you had pictured a wiry, almost spidery man, given to sarcastic smiles, for your villain, when a heavyset, jovial actor may be a better choice. At times, look for *acting ability,* and forget about *type.*

As you interview actors, observe:

- Do they look like the headshot they submitted?
- Do they show the same vitality displayed in the headshot?
- Are there any signs of nervousness, such as tension about mouth and eyes? Are their shoulders tense or hunched? Do they fiddle with jewelry, fingers, or flick off an imaginary fleck of dust from their clothes?
- Do they try to impress you by assuming a phony personality?
- Are they exceedingly timid?

Always look for actors who are relaxed, friendly, and positive about their personal background and achievements. Only the relaxed actors who feel comfortable in an interview situation will be secure in front of the camera. This is an important consideration, since inner tension will make the actor's performance bland or, even worse, "acty." Only *relaxed* actors, who are able to concentrate fully on the task at hand, will give natural and therefore effective on-camera performances.

Have the courtesy to give all the actors you called in the opportunity to read for you. Don't forget, actors are spending their time and money to audition for you, and you never know—one seemingly hopeless actor might surprise you with his or her acting ability. Excerpt short scenes from your script, all applicable to the various parts to be cast. Make plenty of photocopies. Give each auditioning actor the appropriate sides* and plenty of time to study them.

It is best to have your assistant read opposite the actors. This gives you a better opportunity to observe an actor's performance. At the initial reading *do not* expect a polished performance. Even more important, *do not* confuse actors by supplying any suggestions, such as, "At the beginning of this scene Millie is kind of apprehensive, but then she gains confidence." Permit actors to let their own creativity soar. By the same token, if the interviewing actress asks how you want her to play this scene, refrain from guiding her, and suggest that she present the scene in any way she sees fit.

The best initial reading is easy, natural, free of any phony theatricality, yet gives an indication of the character to be portrayed. Such a reading communicates the character's opinion and feeling. It has *immediacy;* that is,

*Pages of a script used for auditioning.

it gives the impression that the actor has something to say and demands an answer. Don't be disappointed if only a few readings come up to par. It takes a skilled and experienced actor to give an "easy" reading.

You should expect that some readings will be nothing but a dull mouthing of lines. Others will sound "acty," and quite a few will look and sound more like a stage than a screen performance. And this brings us to the question, "What is considered an effective screen performance?"

To answer this question, let's look at the difference between stage and screen performance. The stage actor reaches the audience *audially* by the spoken text. The screen actor communicates *visually;* words mean relatively little. Thoughts and emotions count on the screen. Both have to be executed simply and honestly. The camera catches the phony emotion as well as the bland excuse for one.

Most actors auditioning for you undoubtedly will have an extensive stage background. For this reason they might either seem "acty" or, trying to be natural, come across as bland and one-dimensional. On the other hand, the actor who is *only* camera trained is innocent of the most rudimentary acting techniques. You may venture to cast such an actor if you have sufficient off-set rehearsal time. Lacking rehearsal time, this actor might require too much of your personal attention during the shoot and will slow down the production.

CALLBACKS

You will call back actors who:

> Have been relaxed during the initial interview.
> Have given a *fairly* satisfying reading, even if it was a
> little bland or acty.
> Do look *somewhat* the part.

Permit *all* actors to take their audition sides home, and call the ones whom you wish to see again for a callback. These actors hopefully will have worked on their scene. A number of the readings will have improved; others may turn out bland. You never know.

Once you have settled on three to five actors to be considered for the more important roles, you are ready to videotape. This session is the most telling part of your interview sequence, and definitely the most rewarding. Only the camera reveals a person's true personality, or charisma. And as we know, it is charismatic actors who pull the audience into their spell.

At times an actor whose reading was acceptable but not exciting will blossom in front of the camera. The actor who is most effective in front of the camera realizes that the camera is not a piece of equipment, it does not stand in the place of a person, it *is* a person.

The effective motion picture actor:

Communicates with the camera.
Knows how to move in front of a camera.
Has a facial expression (in CU) that is neither dull nor
    overly animated.
Above all, has the *personality* that fills the screen.

After some trial and error you will have assembled your cast. It is a grand day when you finally look at the tapestry of your cast in which each actor complements the rest of your cast, yet still stands out individually. (This holds true for the leading characters as well as for the small parts.)

The Director Creates the Character

The desire to be moved emotionally is your audience's main, if subconscious, reason for attending a movie. Always be aware of the significance of character delineation and development. Remember, you do not tell your audience whether a character is good, bad, or indifferent; you *show* them so they can judge for themselves.

The audience's emotion toward a character is created step by step, as the result of thoughtful and deliberate characterization. Character traits, whether admirable or despicable, are messages that call forth the viewer's emotion, and for this reason they must be shown in action (what characters *do* is more important than what they *say*).

Before you begin rehearsing your actors I recommend that you give close consideration to the characterization of each role. True, you should incorporate whatever your cast has brought in during interviews and callbacks. But do not leave the task of characterization entirely up to your actors.

The individual actor, naturally, is primarily concerned about his or her role, while you, the director, have to consider the tapestry of your entire motion picture.

It is through your own understanding of life that you will create characters who move your audience emotionally. Characterization based on this understanding will keep you from falling into the trap of creating cliché characters. This does not mean that you will bring truly living human beings on the screen. The people we meet in everyday life have so many unrelated traits that, if a director were to try to bring them all to the screen, he or she would succeed only in confusing the audience. In this respect you present to your audience the illusion of life.

Characters are divided into three types:

Simple character
Complex character
Flat character

Simple Character   This character has *one* dominant character trait. Other character traits have to be in accordance with the main character trait, and as such must complement it. You will use the simple character in a *film of purpose,* such as action or adventure films. The *dominant character trait* drives the character to achieve his or her purpose. Do not attempt to give this character a contradictory character trait, or you will weaken the narrative purpose. The simple character is *always* one of your lead actors.

For example, Bill's wife was killed by a gang, and he sets out to avenge her:

Dominant character trait: Loyalty
Secondary character traits: Humor and perseverance

Complex Character   This character has *two contradictory character traits.* Like the simple character, the complex character has some other traits in the background. The complex character has to decide between courses of action, as the contradictory traits pull him or her in two different directions. Both traits have to be developed with equal strength. The complex character is always *the* lead character of a motion picture based on psychological drama.

For instance: Bill has been married to Mary for a number of years; they have two children. They had married very young and now have grown apart, while their marriage has become a marriage of convenience. Bill's professional life is equally stagnant. Even though he has worked hard on his MBA degree, he doesn't get anywhere in the firm he works for. He changes jobs, and meets Belinda, a beautiful young girl. Immediately Bill falls in love. Belinda's father, who owns the company, promises Bill a vice-presidency if he will divorce Mary and marry Belinda. (Yes, I agree, the story sounds as corny as a soap opera, but it serves to make my point:)

Dominant character trait I: Loyalty
Secondary character trait: Honesty
Dominant character trait II: Ambition
Secondary character trait: Pride and sensuality

Flat Character This is always a secondary character. Featured players fall into this category. Most likely it is the flat character who starts the ball rolling. The flat character has only *one* dominant character trait and no secondary character traits. Belinda's father, in our example above, should fall into this category.

Don't forget that secondary character traits make your characters interesting and make them come alive. The character tapestry of our little Bill-Mary-Belinda "soap" might look like this:

Bill: Complex character. Dominant character trait I, Loyalty. Secondary character trait, Honesty. His first dominant character trait keeps him in his marriage. His honesty makes him confess about his love for Belinda. His second dominant character trait makes him consider Belinda's father's proposal. His pride and sensuality make Belinda a prized possession.

Mary: Simple character. Dominant character trait, Love of home and family. Secondary character trait, Courage.

Belinda: Simple character. Dominant character trait, Willfulness. Secondary character traits, Narcissism and sensuality.

Belinda's father: Flat character. Dominant character trait, Love of power.

Looking at this list, you will agree that only one character, the star, should have contradictory character traits.

My advice to you, the beginning director, is that you have a firm grip on the characterization of your various characters *before* you go into rehearsal. Nothing, and I mean nothing, makes an actor more uneasy than a director's vague concept of the characters in a film. Unfortunately, some directors only pay lip service to characterization. They may explain a character this way:

Millie, age 53
Occupation: cashier
Married to a fireman
Two children
She is overworked.
She worries about her children and her husband.

A sketchy characterization like that is a waste of time, and of no help to either you or your actors. So let's consider ways to make characterization work.
Characterization is divided into:

Static characterization
Dynamic characterization
Emotional characterization

STATIC CHARACTERIZATION

The elements making up this type of characterization are:

Lineament (habitual posture, habitual expression)
Occupation/Education
Clothing
Environment
Voice
Health

Lineament   Consider the actors' lines of face and body. Of course, once you have cast an actress to portray one of your film's characters, Millie, these features cannot be changed. But you'll work on the actress's facial expression and her body posture.

Millie forces herself to appear younger than her years.
She works hard on her perpetual sunny smile, erect

posture, and quick, young movements. Her job is important to her, and she has to compete with a number of young, perky girls. Once at home she turns into a middle-aged woman. Her smile is gone, the corners of her mouth turn down, her shoulders sag. She puts on slippers and drags herself from one never-ending household chore to the next. We can tell she is frustrated by the way she bangs her pots and pans around. Her eyes have a far-away look. She worries about her husband, who works too hard, about her married daughter, who is expecting another child, and her son, who never seems able to finish college.

Occupation/Education Millie works as a cashier in a supermarket. She enjoys the hustle and bustle of the store, but is afraid that she may be replaced by a younger girl.

Occupation is an excellent way to come closer to a character's *core*. A college professor will not only have different characteristics from, say, an army officer, truck driver, or musician, but will solve problems by different means, and will react to situations in different ways.

Millie, who has been a cashier from the time she graduated from high school, reacts quickly to any given situation. She is not, however, accustomed to thinking things out, nor does she look for the hidden reason behind someone's action. Moreover, she takes everything at face value.

Clothing Audiences deduce a great deal about a person by what the person wears (approximate cost of clothing, style or lack of style, color, cleanliness, suitability for the person and/or the occasion).

Unfortunately, Millie is given to wearing garments that are more suitable for a younger woman. She is fond of showy jewelry. Her hair is dyed bright blond, and she spends a small fortune on sculptured, brightly painted nails.

Environment   Since we already discussed the importance of environment in chapter 4, suffice it to say that a character is in either harmony or conflict with his or her environment and reacts accordingly.

> Millie liked the excitement and ever-changing display
> of her workplace. Home is another story. She and Sam,
> her husband, have lived in the same house amidst the
> same furniture and bric-a-brac for years. At times Millie
> "hankered to get something new," but now she has
> forgotten about "redoing the place." In fact, she is
> hardly aware of anything in her house. Her home has
> utilitarian value only.

Voice   A character's voice and way of speaking is another excellent tool for characterization. Granted, your actors have to speak *naturally,* but they have to speak as characters of their age, educational level, and socioeconomic background should speak.

> Millie's voice is rather harsh. There is even a nasal
> twang to it.

Health   Don't skip health, as it may give you some clues to dynamic characterization.

> Millie's general health is good, even though she has
> reached an age where her feet and her back hurt as she
> stands at her cash register.

DYNAMIC CHARACTERIZATION

The way a character moves and gestures, the way he or she handles props, establishes dynamic characterization. In other words, characters express themselves by physical action. For instance Alex, whom you wish to portray as a meticulous young man, will pack his suitcase very differently from Nancy, the scatterbrain.

Dynamic characterization applies as well to a character's behavior and attitude when faced with different situations. Brad, the young executive, behaves differently when taking lunch with Mrs. Murdock, his boss, than the way he acts when bowling with his buddies.

EMOTIONAL CHARACTERIZATION

Here, I suggest you characterize sharply. No fuzzy attitudes or phony feelings should crop up on the screen as you show a character's outlook on life. Emotional characterization gives you, the director, the opportunity to manipulate by stressing the character's *dominant emotion*. The dominant emotion refers to the combination of mental and emotional attitudes. Here are but a few examples:

> Mental: intelligence, attitudes, and opinions about life
> and people.
> Emotional: desires, moods, displays of affection or
> dislikes, aggressiveness, submissiveness.
> Millie is an outgoing but rather humdrum person.
> She is of average intelligence, and her philosophy of
> life is "live and let live." She never held book learning
> in high esteem, and she does not understand her son's
> quest for knowledge. She is aggressive with her
> children but submissive with her husband. She is given
> to quick mood swings. No burning desires guide her
> life.

Rehearsals

Compared to the stage director, you the motion picture director have only a limited time available for rehearsals. At times you'll have the luxury to rehearse a few days before shooting; at other times, because of budget restrictions or the availability of key actors, you'll have to rehearse on the set. The time spent on rehearsals varies with each production.

Some actors favor rehearsals; others abhor the idea. The ones who favor rehearsals like to have the entire script "down" on the first shooting day. Those who oppose rehearsals claim that first impulses and intuitions, both creating a gripping performance, tend to get lost during the rehearsal period. Both opinions have their pros and cons. What it boils down to is the fact that you, the director, must be able to *understand, motivate,* and *control* your actors, regardless of whether you rehearse off or on the set.

A delicate combination of control and sensitivity on the part of the director is needed when dealing with actors. Primarily, you'll have to give your actors *security*. Some actors are subconsciously afraid that the director will not be able to control their performances sufficiently. Some, considering the director nothing but a traffic cop who determines camera moves and setups, will call in a lackluster performance or, even worse, ham it up. A few, rejoicing about the director's insecurity, will try to take over.

Know *precisely* what you want; have a clear idea about your motion picture's concept. Have enough sensitivity to listen to your actors' suggestions. If possible, refrain from giving your actors line readings such as, "Please, Janice, read that line this way," or "Do me a favor, Ben, and emphasize this word." Don't forget, actors are professionals; they know what to do, and any amateurish attempt at coaching will meet with strong resistance on their part. Yes, control your actors' goals, motives, and reactions, but never direct their lines. If you do, you may lose their respect.*

The rehearsal period should be used by the director to introduce the actors to their respective characters:

- Decide what makes a character function (goal).
- Decide *why* a character behaves in a certain way during a certain situation (action).
- Define relationships between characters.

Granted, there are some actors who are set against any psychological probing. There is not much you can do about it; either replace the actors in question, or make clear to them that a good motion picture is more than mere words and gestures.

On the other hand, never overdo your rehearsal. Don't freeze your actors into line deliveries or emotions. Most important, do not try to block any scene during off-set rehearsals. Wait until you are on the set or location to make your actors move in front of the camera.

*Consult *How to Audition for Movies and TV,* by Renée Harmon (New York: Walker & Co., 1992).

When rehearsing with actors, always remind yourself of Stanislavsky's statement, "The material of the director's creativity is the creativity of the actor."* This does not necessarily imply that you should not *guide* your actors. After all, Stanislavsky also said, "Acting is neither fixed nor static. Acting is a process, and process implies change."† Therefore you, the director, should demand that the actors understand their roles in terms of the content of your motion picture. Firmly remaining within the narrative boundaries of the film, you should help your actors to reach for their own explanations and observations. Try not to force your own ideas upon them, but compare your ideas with theirs. Be sensitive to your actors' needs. This means you should never expect a specific emotion to be delivered in a specific way.

As far as rehearsals are concerned, do not expect to see a finished performance in the first rehearsal. Give your actors time to explore and to experiment. (This, unfortunately, does not hold true for on-set rehearsals, where you should expect and demand a polished performance. And this is why, if possible, you should opt for an off-set rehearsal period.) Emotions, honestly expressed, require the process of a chain of motives and reactions — that is, a specific circumstance (motive) causing a specific action leads to a specific emotion.

MOTIVE: A CAR CUTS IN FRONT OF YOU

leads to	Physical sensation:	a knot in your stomach
leads to	Physical action:	you step on the brakes
leads to	Thought:	(unprintable)
leads to	Speech:	"Idiot!"

The logical chain of action and emotion often cannot be established because of the obstacle of disconnected scenes (we will discuss a solution to this particular problem later on), and therefore should be dealt with sufficiently during rehearsals, regardless of whether the rehearsal takes place off the set or on. Without the basis of this motive-action-emotion chain, even a skilled actor might be tempted to substitute a cliché emotion for an honest one.

*†Stanislavsky, Konstantin. *Creating a Role*. New York: Theatre Arts Books, 1968.

FUSION OF ACTOR AND CHARACTER

The director has to deal with two identities, the *actor's* and the *character's;* the camera captures the *fusion* of the actor's own personality (experiences, behavior, action, and reaction) and the *character as written* (goals, traits) in the script.

Let me explain: Actor Adam Adams has been cast to portray Jeremiah, a stern Puritan elder. If Adam insists on playing *Adam Adams,* who just incidentally wears a seventeenth-century outfit and carries the name of *Jeremiah,* he will be as wrong as if he were to obliterate his own personality in order to portray Jeremiah.

I said "portray," not "become," Jeremiah on purpose. The widespread misconception that an actor loses himself in the part and becomes the character falsely assumes the actor loses control while going into a trancelike state. To be honest, I have never seen an actor go into a trancelike state. I don't believe it exists, except in poorly written novels and screenplays. Yes, the skilled and effective actor will "forget" about himself while working in front of the camera. But this "forgetting" refers to the actor's complete disregard of personal concern and personal prejudices. The actor who forgets himself concentrates to the fullest on the takes at hand. He doesn't want to impress either the director or audience, he doesn't worry about showing emotions or looking great; no, he is fully absorbed with *doing the scene* in front of the camera.

So please don't ever ask an actor to *become the character.*

DIRECTOR-ACTOR RELATIONSHIP

During a rehearsal, regardless of whether off the set or on, the following should occur:

- The actor fulfills the director's demands.
- The director respects the actor's creativity and sensitivity.
- Both director and actor work to achieve the fusion of actor and character as written.

In this sense a true director-actor relationship will be established. Keeping this relationship in mind, *never* permit your actors:

• To *force* an emotion that they don't feel, and cannot justify. When a particular emotion takes place during a particular scene, never ask your actor "What would you feel in this situation?"; ask instead, "What would you *do?*" At times an appropriate physical action will call forth the appropriate emotion. If no emotion should surface, accept the actor's physical action in lieu of it.

• To *inflate* an emotion (fear, joy, anger) by disregarding the motive that causes the emotion. (For instance, the fear a character experiences when sighting a mouse is different from the fear of being chased by a wild bull.)

• To *stereotype* a character by executing gestures and mannerisms that lack logic and/or consistency. In this way the actor presents only a cardboard imitation of a living, breathing character.

• To work on the *effect* of a line instead of the reality of the scene. If this should happen, advise your actor: "Forget about the emotion expressed by the line you speak, but look at various items in your environment and point them out to me, such as: This is a table, this is a chair, this is a carpet. Now go back to the line you had a problem with. Without any emotion, simply stating a fact (as you had done previously while you pointed out the items in this room) speak your lines."

• To bring in a *polished* but *shallow* performance. Such a performance is easily recognized: The actor reads lines in a skilled but lifeless way, does not react to the given situation sufficiently, or does not think and react while the partners speak. You may help by suggesting your actor get off the lines, to paraphrase the text and improvise the situation.

And now to you, the director:

• Do not try to make your actors carbon copies of yourself—how you would speak a line, how you would react to a given situation.

• Do not demonstrate how you would play a scene. (Granted, this is a temptation for the actor-director.) Don't forget, you are different in temperament, facial expression, and vocal quality from the actor performing the part.

• Respect and develop your actors' creativity; only then will you be able to control them.

• Be prepared for an emotional spiral during your rehearsals. Don't worry if scenes that looked so well in the beginning suddenly seem to go down the drain. If you keep your calm and sense of humor, things will pick up again. The great Russian director Vakhtangov put it so well as he wrote to one of his actors: "You got frightened, then gathered your forces and improved. Then, pleased at how well things were going, you wanted to be still better, and began to overact . . ."*

Always remind your actors that *simplicity* is the key to the effective on-screen performance. If the viewer feels that the actor is not acting at all, since everything seems so easy and natural, you the director have done your job well.

IMPROVISATION

If you are faced with continuous rehearsal difficulties, you may try to get your actors back on track by improvising the scenes or segments of scenes that cause uneasiness. But don't permit an improvisation to turn into an empty rehashing of lines and gestures. Instead encourage your actors to search for the inner meaning of situations or relationships. The helpful improvisation permits actors to make contact with one another, and to discover the various characters' open and hidden goals.

Any improvisation intended to lead to an effective screen performance is based on the *authenticity* of feeling.

Actors must talk to each other and gauge their interaction not on the basis of the lines to be memorized, but on the basis of relationships between characters. This means *thoughts* and *opinions* have to run through the listening character's mind. Any response must come as a result of these thoughts. (We will be dealing more thoroughly with the concept of thoughts later on.)

In exploring the effect of each other's presence, actors should ask themselves:

*Handbook of the Stanislavsky Method. New York: Crown Publishers, 1955. "Preparing for a Role" from the diary of E. Vakhtangov.

How does the opposite character appear?

How do characters change?

How do characters influence each other?

Do not permit actors to "act feelings." In fact, ask them to forget about emotions altogether and to concentrate on *goals* (again, we will look more closely at goals a bit later). Let them discover the *open* as well as the *hidden* goals each character deals with.

Ask actors to invent obstacles that will keep their characters from reaching the desired goal.

Give each actor specific tasks that must be accomplished in specific ways. Establish:

Action	*What* I am doing.
Volition	*Why* I am doing it.
Adjustment	*How* I am doing it.

As actors work on their tasks, ask them to concentrate on the *what* of the tasks, never on the *how*. For instance: *Ann smiles at Elmer.* Her goal: I think Elmer is a neat guy. I would like to get to know him.

Action	Ann smiles.
Volition	I want to show Elmer that I like him.
Adjustment	I smile sweetly.

Now, if the actress portraying Ann smiles at her partner because of her goal, she executes the important What in an easy—and therefore effective—way. If, however, she smiles to show off her radiant smile and beautiful white teeth, then she executes the detrimental How, and her performance lacks honesty.

If, even after improvisations, you are unable to break a deadlocked rehearsal, ask yourself:

· Are my expectations too high?

· Am I theorizing too much?

· Have I prepared myself sufficiently as far as characterizations are concerned?

- Am I temperamentally opposed to any actor, and—unknowingly— tormenting him or her?
- Am I restricting the actors' creativity?

At times I have found that seemingly insurmountable rehearsal obstacles were based on an actor's unrecognized body tension. Such body tension manifests itself most likely in stumbling or forgetting lines and actions. The usual remedy of rolling one's head and shoulders does not help; in fact, as it brings tension to the surface, it makes matters worse. My suggestion is: have the actor stop *immediately*. Ask him or her to *forget* about the lines or task, and then *concentrate* on a straight line somewhere in the room, such as a table top, the outline of the camera, or the line where ceiling and wall meet. I have found this exercise—even during shooting—immensely helpful.

There are times when it will be impossible to schedule off-set rehearsals. Even worse, if you were not involved in the casting of the smaller roles, you will meet your "day players" on the day of the shoot. At this point assuredly you are at the mercy of your actors, who (hopefully) are skilled and experienced.

Even if you won't be able to schedule off-set rehearsals, make every effort to meet with your lead actors at least once prior to the shooting date, to discuss story line and characterization of the respective characters.

Regardless of whether you had off-set rehearsals, use the time while lights are being set up to rehearse with your actors:

- Ask the AD (assistant director) to "run lines" with the actors.
- Take a look at the scene and adjust to appropriate levels:
    Reactions
    Emotions
    Interaction between characters
- Block the scene and let your actors walk through it, giving them plenty of opportunity to familiarize themselves with their physical movements and the locations of floor and peripheral marks.*
- Do not ask the actors to act out the scene during the camera

---

Marks: Floor marks (line, T, and X marks) are taped on the floor. Peripheral marks are points the actor can see out of the corner of his/her eyes.

rehearsal. Acting out again and again results in a stilted scene on-camera.

- Ask your actors to keep their performance fresh for the camera.

It is true, time is money. Still, many beginning directors make the mistake of cutting on-set rehearsals too short. Determine *before* you go on the set how much time you should allocate for each camera rehearsal, and incorporate the time into your shooting schedule.

Overcoming the Problem of Disconnected Scenes

Unlike a stage play, a motion picture is not filmed in a straight and logical line from point A to point Z, but is shot as a hodgepodge of unrelated scenes. The stage director, as well as the stage actor, take the development of an *emotional arch* for granted. You, the motion picture director, cannot. You'll have to work with disconnected bits and pieces. For instance:

> Johnny and his bride, Lisa, arrive at their new home in scene one (location: the Smiths' living room). In scene one hundred fifty the marriage has failed, and they are getting a divorce. Lisa, after another bitter argument with Johnny, storms out of the house. On the threshold she meets Bambi, Johnny's new lady-love.

It stands to reason that both scenes will be shot the very same morning. Performing onstage, actors have the opportunity to build their relationship and reactions to each other (the *emotional arch*); on a film production, they don't. Appropriate emotions and behavior have to happen right then and there.

Even worse, the beginning and the end of a highly emotional scene might be shot directly following each other:

> Betty, ready to discuss her decision to leave college, enters her father's office. After a long encounter she

leaves—exhausted and furious, but determined never
to see her father again.

Betty's entrance and exit will be filmed using the same camera setup,
at the door. Since her exit and entrance will be shot back-to-back*, the actress
portraying Betty has no opportunity to react to any event that took place in
the interim.

Without any doubt, it is your responsibility as the director to discuss
with your actors in detail what has gone on before the segment of the scene
to be shot, and what will happen next. This is particularly important if your
actors have to deal with props: Larry will handle his paperwork one way if
he is worried about a forthcoming meeting with his boss, another way if he
is looking forward to a pleasant weekend. Mary Ellen will enter her apartment tired after a hard day's work, or elated after a successful shopping trip.

Always discuss with your actors:

- Where has the character been at the end of the previous scene (or
  segment of a scene)?
- Why was the character there?
- What did the character do there?
- Where will the character be in the following scene?
- What will the character do in the following scene?
- What was the character's relationship to other characters in the
  previous scene? Have any of the relationships changed?
- Discuss how thoughts, feelings, opinions, and attitudes of previous
  scenes will influence the scene to be shot presently.

You, the director who is responsible for the tapestry of your film, should
be fully aware of the *reality* of each scene, and the way each scene, each
event, and each emotion should build on the previous one.

The Scenic Blueprint

Regardless of where you are rehearsing, a scenic blueprint is a must. Your
scenic blueprint is as important as your shooting script. You, the beginning

---

*"Back-to-back" refers to takes or scenes that follow each other immediately.

director, are especially in need of one, as the numerous pressures and dis-
tractions you will encounter on the set—the decisions to be made, the tem-
pers to be calmed—make on-the-spot creativity impossible. The workable
scenic blueprint deals with the following:

Goals
Motive
Relationships
Physical actions
Conditioning forces

GOALS

Emotions, opinions, and relationships are built on goals. In simple terms, a
goal is *what a character wants to achieve.* There is one overall goal that determines all of a character's actions throughout the script (*Snow White:* the
Queen wants to get rid of Snow White), and subgoals within each scene
that lead to the achievement of the overall goal. (First subgoal: the Queen
hires the Hunter to kill Snow White. Second subgoal: she dresses as a peddler
and presents Snow White with a deadly comb. Third subgoal: she hands
Snow White a poisoned apple.)

Each goal should be stated specifically, never generally. As an example,
let's take another look at the little dressing room scene (page 79) and the
individual goals it contains:

Claudia wants to *revive* her career.
Ralph wants to *help* Claudia.
Al wants to *orchestrate* Claudia's career.

As you can see, each goal is stated clearly and therefore understandably for
the audience. One knows what each character *wants.* None of the goals has
been stated in a general way, such as, "Claudia is angry because she's worried about her career," "Ralph feels sorry for Claudia," or "Al is enthusiastic
about getting Claudia's career back on the right track." You can tell, stating
a goal in a general way tells about the respective characters' emotions, *not*
about their actions. *Physical* (what a character does) and *mental* (what a char-

acter desires) *actions* are the foundation of simple and honest acting. The keys to arriving at clearly stated—and therefore actable—goals are:

Keep your goal sentence short.
State "I want to"—followed by a verb.
Claudia: I want to *revive* my career.
Ralph: I want to *help* Claudia.
Al: I want to *orchestrate* Claudia's career.

In developing a goal, make certain that the goal is based on each character's *desire* as well as the *motive* that caused the desire. And this brings us to *open* and *hidden* goals.

Take another look at the dressing room scene. You will agree with me that, even though the given goals are actable, they will not make for a captivating scene. Too bad; after all, this scene sets the film's events in motion. So, what happens in this scene? Claudia, Ralph, and Al all decide to revive Claudia's career. *To revive* is the scene's open goal, which—unfortunately—does not carry much creative power. The director's and the actors' artistic opportunity lies in each character's hidden goal.

The open goal states *what a character does,* and the hidden goal reveals *why a character acts in a certain way.*

It is the *hidden goal* that is the true reason behind a character's open goal and his or her resulting actions. The hidden goal adds color and depth to the actor's performance. Hidden goals will make the bland dressing room scene interesting. So, here we go:

Claudia *What is she doing?* She wants to establish her power over Al and Ralph. *How is she doing it?* She uses her wiles. Hidden goal: I want to enjoy the power I hold over Ralph and Al.

Ralph *What is he doing?* He wants to remain in Claudia's good graces. *Why is he doing it?* He is afraid of losing Claudia to Al. Hidden goal: I want to show Claudia that I am caring and reliable.

Al *What is he doing?* He wants to show Claudia that he is her boss. *Why is he doing it?* He needs to revive Claudia's career, because she is his meal ticket. Hidden goal: I want to show Claudia that she is nothing without me.

MOTIVE

In order to arrive at a goal, a character must have a motive. Webster defines *motive* as "to supply with a reason to move." Your script gives your characters basic problems and the ways they try to solve them. You and your actors are responsible for the motivational interplay, which, to be sure, must be based on reasonable motives.

The motive is the springboard for mental and physical goals and physical action. All motives are based on human urges:

The life urge	Self-preservation, preservation of others, fear, hunger.
The sex urge	Love, loyalty, sexual drive.
The power urge	Construction and destruction, the desire to better self or others, control.
The creative urge	Creativity in all its forms.

Motives form relationships, or in case a relationship has been established, a motive may change the relationship. And from here, quite naturally, we will concern ourselves with relationship.

RELATIONSHIPS

If you want to bring electrifying relationships to the screen, you must set characters against one another. This does not indicate that you have to pit one character against another, that characters must fight or become involved in biting discussions, but it means that you, the director, have to be very much aware of *changes* in relationship. Relationships are never static. Characters come together or they move apart:

COMING TOGETHER

Initiating	Characters show their interest in each other. Putting his best foot forward, a character will initiate a relationship: "Hi, how are you?"

Experimenting   Characters begin to search for common interests, opinions, and beliefs. "You like the beach?" "I adore the beach, do you like to visit museums?"

Intensifying   Now characters know each other, and a desire for commitment arises. "I am so happy we met." "Nothing better ever happened to me."

Bonding   Characters become partners. They get married, move in together, or—on an unemotional level—form a business or political partnership.

COMING APART

Differentiating   After characters have bonded, they will establish their individuality. This, basically, is a healthy process that may either deepen a relationship or be the cause for an eventual breakup.

Stagnating   Characters treat each other without much feeling. They are bored. "How are things at the office?" "Fine, when will dinner be ready?"

Avoiding   When a relationship becomes unpleasant, characters tend to avoid each other.

Terminating   The relationship dissolves.

The relationship stages in your film, of course, are never as cut-and-dried as the above list suggests. Your script's dialog may not even touch on them, but the *feeling* is beneath the lines. Search for it, dig it out, and let your actors express it in thoughts and physical actions.

As far as relationships in all stages are concerned, one partner leads, the other follows. Positions in relationships are characterized by the way characters *communicate* with each other. Generally we find two basic communication patterns:

- One partner consistently overpowers the other.
- Power is fairly evenly distributed between partners, or tends to shift according to different situations.

The way characters communicate with each other is not necessarily spelled out in the written dialog of your script, and therefore it ought to be shown in each character's tone of voice, attention or inattention to the partner, and physical actions.

Once a basic relationship has been established, search for the telling details. Isolate moments in the relationship that will challenge, surprise, elate, or worry your characters, and find the appropriate expression for them.

PHYSICAL ACTIONS

Physical actions *must* arise from a goal, based on a motive—not the vague feeling, "It's time that I move my actors around." Communication established via physical action is one of the most powerful acting tools if—and only if—the actor believes fully in, and concentrates on, the physical action as he executes it. The actress ironing a pleated shirt should not *act* ironing but concern herself with doing the very best ironing job she can, carefully first straightening, then dampening, and finally ironing each pleat.

Decisions about physical actions (not to be confused with blocking) should be made when you write your shooting script. If you wait until you are on the set, the physical actions might turn into a general rehash of things you have done or seen before, instead of the character-revealing signals they are supposed to be. Therefore it will serve you and your actors well if you write a list of physical actions.

For purposes of illustration we will go again (for the last time, I promise) to our friends Claudia, Ralph, and Al, to find out how physical actions are based on each character's hidden goal.

LIST OF PHYSICAL ACTIONS—CLAUDIA

Claudia, seated at her dressing table, checks her perfect makeup. She brushes off a speck of powder, dabs on a little more rouge, and all the time admires herself. Completely absorbed in her task, she seems oblivious of both Al and Ralph.

She brushes Ralph's attention off. She is used to him. Maybe she is even getting a little bored by his considerate behavior.

When she finally stoops to give Al's suggestions a

fleeting thought and word, she gazes at him with looks that could freeze a polar bear. Immediately dismissing Ralph and Al, she walks to the costume rack. Examining her costumes, she indicates that these are more important than either Ralph or Al.

Having chosen an appropriate outfit, Claudia takes it off the rack and moves back to her dressing table.

Finally, wielding the power of her charm and beauty, she rewards her vassals with one of her radiant, and famous, smiles.

LIST OF PHYSICAL ACTIONS — RALPH

Whenever possible Ralph sidles up to Claudia. Like a barnacle he attaches himself to her. His sweet, subservient smile seems to be glued on his face. If he is unable to follow Claudia physically, he follows her with the trusting, begging eyes of a Saint Bernard rescue dog.

Whenever Al speaks to him, Ralph's head twitches to the side, and his shoulders pull forward protectively.

As soon as Al moves close to Claudia, Ralph takes up his guard post next to her.

LIST OF PHYSICAL ACTIONS — AL

Al is constantly on the move. His posture is erect. He makes certain that whenever he makes a point, he towers over Claudia. As far as Ralph is concerned, Al could not disregard him less. He hardly ever looks at him.

CONDITIONING FORCES

Inherent in any story are the conditions of time, place, and climate, as well as any obstacles that may be associated with them.

Time Elements that are not directly stated in the script can be established through references to time. Many beginning directors, unfortunately, disregard the implications of time, or consider only the obvious aspects of it. Yet in many ways time influences the opinion, behavior, and ethics of the characters you have to create for the screen.

For example, let's say that the subplot of your film deals with the relationship between Lucy, a young woman, and Homer, a married man. It is 1798. The French Revolution has swept away all social and religious restrictions. Personal freedom is the buzzword of the time. Lucy and Homer are seen together everywhere. They flaunt their affair as they attend the opera together and patronize the most fashionable Paris restaurants. Everyone invites them, no one cares about their illegitimate relationship — even Homer's wife (she has a lover of her own) couldn't care less. She and Lucy are dear friends.

If the story is set fifty years later, things have changed considerably. Queen Victoria graces the British throne, and her own rigid moral behavior has become society's measuring tape. Yet behind this facade of stern respectability hovers a shackled and therefore morbid sexuality. Homer, the respected citizen, rules wife, children, and servants with an iron hand. His sweetly submissive wife suspects he has a mistress but never dares to mention her. Homer visits Lucy, his "Lady Love," on the sly. They are never seen together, and only Homer's closest, most discreet friends know about Lucy's existence.

Then we rewrite to 1970. Free love reigns. Lucy, a professional woman, can afford an expensive foreign car. She lives in a penthouse and prefers to buy designer outfits. She also can afford to have one affair after the other. She discards lovers as casually as her clothes that are out of style. Homer is just one of her lovers. He knows it and expects that one of these days Lucy will leave him, as he has left the hat-check girl he had seen for a while.

And then, without anyone noticing, it is 1990. People are afraid of casual encounters. Relationships that depend on emotional involvement have become important again. Lucy and Homer are deeply in love, and for this very reason complications arise. Lucy wants a home and a family of her own, but Homer is reluctant to ask his wife for a divorce. He doesn't love her anymore, but he is attached to her, and loves his two children. A divorce would tear his family and comfortable surburban life apart. And anyway, who wants to pay child support and alimony?

Not only does time apply to the ethical and moral atmosphere of a period, it also very specifically defines part of the day. In this respect time governs the way characters move and behave.

Mark, getting up early in the morning, will lumber slowly to the coffeepot to pour the first reviving cup of the day. Yet he will move quickly and efficiently as he waits on the customers in his father's hardware store. In the evening, with the TV remote control in hand, he stretches comfortably on the couch.

Ella, the intern, moves more efficiently during the afternoon. At night, after she has been on duty for hours, her movements are sluggish.

Consider, too, the amount of time it takes characters to accomplish a given task. For example, Betty will spend far less time combing her hair and applying makeup when she gets ready to go to work than when she is preparing for an important date.

Place   As we have discussed in the previous chapter, characters are either in harmony or in conflict with their environment (place) and must react to it accordingly.

Climate   Make your actors aware of the climate of particular scenes. (It never fails; by some quirk of fate beach scenes are shot in freezing cold weather. And in August, I bet, you will be shooting a scene that takes place on an icy mountaintop in the middle of winter. Moreover, the set has been constructed on a stage that of course lacks air-conditioning.)

Climate affects the rhythm of characters' movement and speech. It changes body posture and at times is responsible for mood swings and variations.

I know you'll agree with me about the influence that the various conditioning forces exert. Conditioning forces give the actors the impetus to move, speak, act, and react in certain ways; they add to the reality of a scene; but they do *not* constitute the scene per se. For this reason, don't permit conditioning forces to overpower a scene or confuse your audience with unnecessary details.

The Director's Creative Safeguard

It might happen to you: you started out with a solid script, wrote a thorough shooting script, worked diligently on camera setups and moves, found terrific locations, cast skilled and talented actors and rehearsed with them, supervised postproduction—in short, you did everything according to plan, and yet finally you were forced to watch a movie that was not really *satisfactory*.

Yes, it can happen. It happened to me.

So, what went wrong?

In the excitement of creating the characters on the screen you, and to a lesser degree your actors, have moved too far from the characters as written in the script. Remember, the character seen on the screen must be a fusion of the character as written and the actor's own personality. It's likely that the two most vital components of your film—*script* and *acting*—do not quite fit. Note that I said, do not *quite* fit, and this makes a difference. Your movie is all right, but not quite as exciting as you had envisioned it, because its *narrative logic* is slightly off balance. You strayed too far from the characters as depicted in the script; in other words, the goals and ensuing actions of the characters on the screen do not quite fit the motives given in the script. Yes, your actors' responsibility is to breathe life into the characters, but neither you nor your actors should change them.

Unfortunately, in the heat of creation subtle changes—which turn out to be monsters later on—remain undetected. To prevent such mistakes, it might be a good idea to employ, prior to rehearsal, the device of "facts and conclusions," a technique actors have used for a long time. It works like this: Perusing your entire script, you make a list for each of the leading characters:

What the character says about himself or herself.
Appropriate stage directions.
What other characters say about him or her.

You list all the facts you have found, and next to them you write your conclusions. But be careful (and this is where creativity often goes astray): stick with the *given* facts first, then tack on your conclusions. Granted, the fact and assumption search is a tedious job, but it pays off in the end with motivated characters who follow a clear goal, since the totality of facts and conclusions gives an excellent picture of the character as written.

We'll use one of the beginning scenes from my film *Four Blind Mice* as an example:

Exterior Park. Day. Early Morning.

(It is a seemingly cold, slightly foggy fall morning. The camera [various angles] takes in the group of homeless people having taken shelter in the park. Most of them are still asleep.

Cut to AHNA's *car, a dilapidated old vehicle overflowing with her poor possessions. There are bags and cardboard boxes. Some old clothing has been spread on the hood of the car. There are pots and pans, an old calendar has been taped to one of the windows. The car doors are open.* AHNA *is busy with her "household chores."* ART, *an elderly homeless man, leans against one of the doors.)*

ART: You should go with me to the mission—nice people, and the food is good. Well, you'll have to listen to a preacher, but who cares . . .

AHNA: Maybe . . .

ART: Come on . . . why not.

*(*AHNA, *afraid to hurt his feelings, hesitates.)*

ART: 'Cause it's a handout. Woman, you have much to learn. We all have to accept . . . what you call it?

AHNA: Charity.

ART: Yeah, charity . . . how long have you been on the streets?

*(*AHNA *tries to remember. She has difficulty stringing one thought on the next.)*

AHNA: They let me go at the hospital . . .

ART: The nuthouse?

*(*AHNA *nods. She counts on her fingers.)*

AHNA: Mhm . . . I guess that was in May . . . the sun was shining, and the flowers on the matron's windowsill were in bloom . . . I went back home . . . I can't remember when. I was in this apartment . . . but then my money ran out and they evicted me . . . I have been on the streets for about three months . . . *(now positive)* . . . yes, three months.

ART: You are still green, but you'll learn, you'll get with it.

FACTS	CONCLUSIONS
1. Ahna lives in a park in an old car.	1. Ahna is homeless.
2. Her car is overflowing with her possessions.	2. Compared with the other homeless who sleep in cardboard boxes, she is still "well off."
3. She hesitates to hurt Art.	3. She is sensitive.
4. She refuses to go to the mission for a handout.	4. She has pride, and possibly some money to buy her food.
5. She was in a mental institution.	5. She is either mentally or emotionally ill.
6. She lived in an apartment after her release.	6. There was some money she lived on.
7. She was evicted.	7. She has no one who takes care of her.
8. She is still new on the streets.	8. She has much to learn, and much to adjust to. Life on the streets is still new, and probably frightening for her.

THE DIRECTOR'S REHEARSAL BLUEPRINTS

For you, the beginning director, it might be a good practice to write out characterization and scenic blueprints, to serve you as creative springboards during rehearsal and shooting.

The characterization blueprint (for leading characters only) should contain the following information:

COMPLEX OR SIMPLE CHARACTER:

Dominant character trait(s)
Secondary character trait(s)
(Both traits cannot clash with the motive given in the
   script).

Static characterization:
    Lineament (habitual posture, facial expression)
    Occupation
    Clothing
    Environment
    Voice
    Health

Dynamic Characterization:
    Emotional characterization
    Mental attitudes
    Emotional attitudes

The scenic blueprint should contain the following:

Motives
Goals
State of relationships
Conditioning forces:
    Time
    Place
    Climate
    Obstacles

6.

Dialog

We have already discussed the problems of dialog in the motion picture, and the fact that clearly expressed emotions arouse the audience. The audience reacts more to what it *sees* than what it *hears*. Consequently, important information and character detail may be unclear to the viewers unless you, the director, are able to draw their attention to what characters *say* as well as what they *do*. This, I warn you, will happen only if the spoken word is carried by honest and simply expressed emotions. All of us—you and I, the audience and the characters on the screen—exist most vitally in the world of emotions. Therefore no fuzzy dialog is allowable if you wish to create a full emotional effect. Always consider, the emotions felt by the protagonists on the screen are the emotions that ought to be felt simultaneously by the viewer. For this reason, remind your actors:

- Dialog shows character.
- Dialog shows the emotional state of the characters.
- Dialog not only gives information; by the way the actors deliver their lines, it has to build suspense.

Be careful that no two of your characters speak alike. For instance, in a discussion between two corporate lawyers, the dialog as written in your script sounds pretty much alike, the facts they are discussing are rather hum-drum, yet are important for the picture's story line.

You will make Roger McGowan and Charlie Reynolds, his partner, much more palatable by characterizing their dialog. Make Roger a stickler for detail. Give him a pointed and precise speech pattern, let him emphasize his contentions by pointing a pencil whenever he hits a mental obstacle. Add to all of this his quick head and hand movements, and you'll show a truly stinging man.

In contrast, make Charles a jovial kind of person. Permit him to loll in his chair, smile, shrug his shoulders as he accentuates his slowly delivered but well-thought-out arguments with rounded hand movements.

Even the way a character delivers as bland a line as "I guess it will rain tomorrow" identifies that character as kind, angry, bitchy, shy, phony, elated, compassionate. In short, effective line delivery encompasses the entire spec-trum of human emotions. Therefore don't ever permit actors to "read lines," which refers to a stilted dialog delivery. Likewise, do not condone any bland or lackluster line interpretation. Dialog has to show color as it conveys a character's opinions and emotions.

When it comes time to rehearse both off the set and on, be cognizant that all of us have different *vocabularies*. We speak differently to a teenager, the plumber who fixes our leaking kitchen faucet, the boss who calls us in for a conference, a friend we share a leisurely lunch with. While writers and directors are well aware of the vocabulary differences among different socio-economic groups, they often disregard *tonal shift* that determines dialog between characters. These delicate shifts are impossible to discern in the script, and only rehearsal will open everyone's ears to them.

Tonal shift also applies to the meaning behind the spoken lines. Elinor's line, "Are you planning to play tennis next Saturday?" will sound different if she:

Suspects John of having an affair with Linda.
Wants to go to a movie if John plans to play tennis.
Wants to make small talk.

Furthermore, be aware of sentence structures that *read* well but do not *speak* well. The following line does not read too poorly, but try to speak it, and immediately your speech sounds phony: "It was a lovely morning. I played a round of golf and then went for a swim in the lake." Now try this: "Great morning. Chased a few balls around the course and took a dip in the lake."

At times you may not become aware of stilted sentences until rehearsal. If a skilled actor delivers a line in a theatrical way, don't blame it on the actor, but rewrite the line.

The *speed* at which a character talks, the *spacing* and *physical actions* that separate words or sentences, are sound indicators of a character's personality:

Kathy keeps on ironing as she says briskly:

"No, I have not seen Robert for some time. It has been about a year since I met him at a teacher's convention. Any reason why you ask?"

or:

"No."

Carefully Kathy spreads a pillowcase over the ironing board. She looks up:

". . . It has been about a year . . ."

Kathy begins to iron.

". . . since I met him at a teachers' convention."

Kathy continues to iron. She inspects a rip in the pillowcase before she — unexpectedly — explodes:

"Any reason why you ask?"

Watch carefully, or you will have every character on the screen talking alike. Your audience wants contrast in everything, including the dialog on the screen.

All of the above means that you should do thorough characterization work *before* you start rehearsals (but after you have cast your actors), in which you'll have to consider a character's age, emotional state, cultural and socio-economic background, as well as his or her basic personality.

During rehearsals listen to your actors. Watch their facial expressions and bodily movements, for it is the way in which a character operates that characterizes him or her. And don't forget to concentrate your attention on the way your actors express their thoughts.

The skillful application of thoughts greatly enhances any screen performance. This is yet another reason why you, the director, should choose experienced motion picture actors over stage actors. Whereas stage actors are concerned primarily with words, the screen actor is fully aware of the importance of thought expression:

> Always have your characters think under stress.
> If at all possible, get conflict into a character's thinking
> process.

Technically, thoughts may be expressed:

> Before a line.
> In the middle of a line.
> After a line.

A thought leads into a line and as such causes a character's emotion:

Thought: Finally I can take a few days off. What a relief.
Line: "Tomorrow we're going on vacation."

A thought might oppose the spoken line:

Thought: What a waste of time and money.
Line: "Tomorrow we're going on vacation."

A thought might be stronger in emotional content than the spoken line:

Thought: If I don't get away, I'll collapse.

Actors must think dynamic thoughts while their partner speaks. The listening actor's thoughts are the springboard (motive) for any spoken or physically expressed answer.

Thoughts, like dialog, must be in character. Cedric, who weighs his words carefully, will think differently from Ralph, whose opinions tumble out in unrelated sentences.

Always ask your actors to *think real thoughts;* do not permit them to stare soulfully into empty space.

Part Four

7.

Postproduction

The film has been shot, it is "in the can," but your responsibility has not yet ended. Some directors even contend that the most crucial work begins *in the editing room.* Fortunate is the director who possesses a solid editing background, but every director—whether from the writing, acting, or producing side—should have at least some basic knowledge of the editing process. No matter how experienced your editor is, do not turn over your film to him or her indiscriminately, or you may find its rhythm has been changed, its style has been distorted. On the other hand, do not expect a film editor to save a hopeless movie. (The miracle of *High Noon,* wherein the editor literally saved the motion picture from destruction, happens only once in a blue moon.) You should, of course, expect that minor flaws will be taken care of:

- A faulty line can be corrected by substituting the same track from a different take (one of the reasons that even though the first take is perfect, you should shoot another one for security).
- If an actor's performance is not quite up to your standards, you can substitute another actor's reaction over this actor's lines.

- A "wild line" (a line recorded after the movie has been finished) can be added wherever deemed necessary.

To put it simply, editing is the process of cutting a film from one shot to the next in such a way as to give the audience the illusion of continuous action. Like camera movement, every cut should follow the *narrative logic* of your film.

Editing the Picture

During the production time, each day's output of exposed film, the "dailies" or "rushes," will be developed by the lab. You'll receive a "1 light" print, which, while the original footage is stored in the lab's vault serves as a work print, the print your editor edits.

The following are the stages a film moves through from the dailies to the answer print:

- *Dailies:* Each day's footage should be spliced together. Some directors omit this step, but I feel that splicing dailies together helps to keep the avalanche of exposed film in some kind of order.
- *Rough cut:* Scenes are strung together in appropriate order. The film is still uneven, in some parts too long, others too short or illogical. In this way you can evaluate strong and weak points.
- *First assembly:* The film's weak points need to be corrected, and its final length has to be established.
- *Three-quarter cut:* The film is now fairly smooth in appearance, and the sound editing has been completed.
- *Final cut:* Even though the "final cut" shows the supposedly final version of your film, some minor changes are still possible. By now picture and sound tracks can be run in interlock—that is, film and sound will be projected from different sources.
- *Negative cut:* Once your final cut has been struck, the original footage will be edited based on it.
- *Answer print:* This print is struck from the negative cut. If you so desire, you still can change a thing here or there. I would,

however, strongly advise against this money-wasting practice.
Decide on changes while cutting your final cut.

And now let's take a look at the equipment your editor needs to cut
the picture.

- *Moviola:* The Moviola is the standard editing machine. It consists of
  a motorized viewer and sound system. Sound head and viewer
  head are interlocked so they run together.
- *Splicers:* Mylar splice, perforated
  Mylar splice, unperforated (guillotine)
  Cement splice

Mylar Splice   The Mylar splice requires a far less skilled editor than the
cement splice, and it can be made much faster. It is the preferred method
for cutting dailies and the rough cut. A Mylar tape very much like an ordinary
type of tape is placed across the cut on both sides. It can be removed easily,
but will—since it is thicker than the film—throw the image somewhat out
of focus as the film moves through the projector gate.

Guillotine Splice   This is an excellent method for the skilled editor, who
works quickly and efficiently with the unperforated guillotine tape. Guillotine
splicing is most effectively used for sound editing.

Cement Splice   A cement splice should be used for the negative cut. A
cement splice is made by overlapping two sections of film. The base of one
cut is dissolved into the base of the next, so the two sections become one.
If the editor is not skilled in this splicing technique, the overlap becomes
thicker than the film and will be seen as a distracting flash on the screen.
When using a cement splice you'll lose a frame at the point of cutting and
joining. (For sound editing cement splices should be avoided, since they
cause a drop in the sound level.)

No matter what type of splicing technique the editor employs, he or
she needs storage reels and storage bins, leaders, and—most important—
white gloves. Make certain that your editor handles your film with utmost
care. Dust, scratches, or fingerprints will ruin your film. No film should ever
be wound so tightly as to cause cinch marks. Scratches may have been
created during the editing process, by the camera when the film was shot,

or, even more likely, during development. Base scratches can usually be buffed, but if they are on the emulsion side, obviously there is little anyone can do about them.

Leaders are made of yellowish-white undeveloped film. Leaders are used to mark the *head* (beginning) and *tail* (end) of every roll. Your editor uses a non-water-based marking pen to mark the leader. Leaders are useful for slugging (the replacement of damaged footage).

EDITING AND SPLICING

Even though it is unlikely that you will get hands-on experience, as director you ought to know about editing and splicing techniques.

EDITING

- Rewind the film so that the beginning of the footage is on the outside of the reel.
- Thread the footage and view it.
- Make notes on the intended editing sequence.
- View the film again and start cutting.
- After making cuts, label the individual "clips" with white tape and clamp them on the editing table.
- Keep track of the order of the film clips by listing the scenes on a pad and by marking the clips with corresponding numbers.
- Splice all of the unused takes, the *outtakes,* together. At times during the editing process these outtakes may turn out to be lifesavers.
- Put the film clips together in the order in which they are to be cut.

Splicing needs practice and practice and practice again. Here is how it works:

SPLICING

- Lift the left side of your splicer, and lock your film clip into the right-hand side. The emulsion side of the film must be placed face up.
- Bring down the left side of the splicer and cut the clip.
- Raise the right side of the splicer and lock the other clip into the left side (the emulsion side must face up).

- Bring down the right side and cut the film. Raise the right side again.
- Scrape the emulsion (cement splice technique) and scrape the film.
- Apply cement on the scraped side, bring down the right side, and lock.
- Wait about seven seconds for the cement to dry (a hot splicer will cut down the drying time to about three seconds), then lift the upper half of both sides of the splicer. Wipe off excess cement.
- Remove the film and tug slightly to check whether or not the splice will hold.

CREATIVE EDITING

Now that you have some idea about the mechanical side of cutting (splicing), let's move on and take a look at the more creative side of the process. Let's say you are cutting a dialog between two people, actor A and actor B, as they walk down a busy downtown street. We will have to concern ourselves with:

- Picture
- Sound: Dialog, sound effects, and possibly music.

Run this scene on the Moviola until you get to the point where you want to cut from the Two-Shot into a Reversal of actor A, and mark the spot with a grease pencil on both the picture frame and the sound frame. Lift the material out of the Moviola and cut with scissors. You repeat the same process with actor B's lines, then splice the two cuts together. If picture and sound track have been marked correctly and locked into the Moviola in sync, you will be rewarded with a synchronized scene.

Matters are a little more complicated if you wish to show actor B's reaction over actor A's lines. Let's say you have decided to show forty frames of actor B's reaction while actor A speaks; then you must take forty frames out of the picture shot of A talking. Choose the part of the shot you wish to "over" with B's reaction, cut the picture and corresponding sound track out, replace the forty frames with B's reaction, and place the sound track of actor A's lines "over" B's reaction.

Once the picture and dialog tracks have been cut, you set them aside and put the sound effects and music into place. (We will discuss sound editing in detail next.) On the sound effect and music tracks, the places between effects (where dialog belongs) will be filled in with blank tape. Picture, dialog, sound effects, and music tracks have to be combined later on in a procedure called a *mix*.

SOUND EDITING

Just as you send each day's film footage to the lab for dailies, you will send your recorded sound to a sound lab. The lab transfers the recorded sound (mostly dialog) to 35mm magnetic film (MAG). MAG looks exactly like the raw stock used in your camera, except that the light-sensitive emulsion used on camera film has been stripped and replaced by oxide. There is prestripped film—raw stock with the magnetic stripe already applied—on the market, but I advise against using it. If the magnetic stripe is of inferior quality, it will cause unnecessary wear on your camera.

Ask your producer to use the very best sound lab the budget can afford. At times a poor sound track has ruined an otherwise excellent movie.

The magnetic sound tracks will be returned to your sound editor, who works with at least three sound tracks:

- *Dialog* (Make certain that the dialog track can be removed from your finished film. Foreign buyers will replace it with a sound track of their own.)
- *Sound effects* (these may be on one track, or several)
- *Music*

Your sound editor first cuts the dialog track, then sets music and sound effects in place. You have to watch the continuity of sound effects. For instance, at times sound is more continuous than picture: Mary and Sam attend a lively party, greet their friends Billy and Jo, then move on to meet with their host, Ralph. Every so often we cut back to the waiter Jo, watching what is going on. As we cut from group to group, the entire scene is pulled together by the continuous sound of laughter and talk.

The editor cuts the sound to match the picture. At times he or she *plugs* the picture with leader for a "wild sound," stretches where sound has to be added later.

The sound editor lays the corresponding sound and picture tracks together and places a start mark (X) on the head leader at the point of synchronization. Once your work print has been synchronized, it is a good idea to send it back to the lab for *machine edge numbering.* When picture and sound have corresponding edge numbers, making your negative cut will be easier (and therefore less expensive).

As soon as picture and sound editing has been completed, your film goes back to the sound lab for a mix.

Working with magnetic tape can cause your equipment to become magnetized. Scissors, splicers, recorder heads, and reels may all become magnetized. When scissors and splicers become magnetized, they will add a clicking sound wherever your track has been cut. Magnetized equipment must be *degaussed.* A small pencillike degausser will do the trick.

MIXING

The mixing session is an exciting period. It is now that you view your film with all its component parts together. Mixing sessions, unfortunately, are expensive. Ten minutes of film to be seen on the screen may take from thirty minutes to two hours to mix. For this reason, edit sound and picture meticulously before attempting the mix. Here are some hints that will make mixing a little less intimidating:

- Practice the mix several times before you record one.
- With masking tape make a label next to each volume control: dialog, music, sound effects.
- If you have to choose between clarity of dialog or music (sound effects), choose the former.
- If you are short on tracks, you should use a "tape loop" for a continuous effect such as surf, wind, party, or traffic sounds. A section about three feet long is spliced to its own beginning, forming a loop.

Most dialog is put on either one or two tracks. Separate tracks are used for sound effects, room and/or environmental ambience, and music. A mixer adjusts the levels of each track and equalizes them to get the best results. Whenever one sound melts into another, both sounds must be placed on separate tracks, with one foot *overlap* at least.

Most mixing studios feature a footage counter, and you should supply the person responsible for the mix with a cue sheet indicating at which point the picture track has dialog, sound effects, or music. Make a log that has a column for the picture track and separate columns for each sound track.

Once the mixing session has been completed, the lab will supply you with a ¼" tape of the mix.

OPTICAL TRACK

Next you'll take your ¼" tape to an optical lab to have an optical track made. This lab manufactures a separate film that has no picture image but has the photographic image of your sound along its edge.

You need to know whether you need a negative or positive track:

Black and white negative film—negative optical track
Black and white reversal film—positive optical track
Color negative film—negative optical track
Color reversal stock—negative optical track

The optical track, let me warn you, is expensive, as are all other opticals. The term *opticals* covers:

Optical effects
Many special effects
Titles

Optical Effects Most optical effects are used for transitions between scenes. Since optical effects are expensive, you may well reconsider whether you really need all those effects indicated in the original script. My advice is that while working on your shooting script you eliminate as many optical effects as possible.

- *Fade:* A shot gradually disappears or appears.
- *Dissolve:* Two shots are superimposed. The second shot appears out of the first shot.
- *Wipe:* The second shot pushes the first shot off the screen.
- *Flipover:* The image turns over, revealing what seems to be its other side.

- *Optical zoom:* An area is enlarged progressively. (Since there is always the danger that the picture may appear grainy, it is better—and less expensive—to use a zoom lens whenever a zoom is desired.)
- *Skip framing:* By printing only some of the frames of the original, action is speeded up. Skip framing can be used for comical effects, or—very effectively—for all car chases. If you are doing an action film, skip framing will make a mediocre car chase exciting.
- *Double framing:* Each frame can be printed twice or more to slow the action down. It is, however, less expensive to shoot at higher speed to achieve the same effect.
- *Freeze:* Action is stopped. Freezes are often used at the end of a film to "over" credits. I feel money spent on freeze for end titles is wasted.

Special Effects   Most special effects requiring the services of a lab are too expensive for you, the beginning director. That does not mean that you should stay away from special effects—after all, what is a horror movie without them—but it indicates that you should be aware of ways to bring inexpensive but highly effective special effects to the screen. Chapter 9 will deal with this highly creative part of your work.

Titles   Especially if superimposed over action, titles can be very expensive. To keep costs down to a minimum, you must give your optical house detailed instructions. Do not leave any decisions about titles up to them. Your first trip will be to the title house to have title cards made. Check the spelling of all names carefully, for you do not wish to redo titles. My advice is to stay away from complicated titles. White lettering on a black background always serves well. I like to begin my films with a short action sequence and from there go into simple titles, followed by another sequence of action and the remainder of the titles.

NEGATIVE CUTTING

The negative cutter (I suggest that you employ the most skillful cutter your budget can afford) will match each of the cuts in the work print with the corresponding cuts in the original footage. (Remember, you had corresponding edge numbers printed on both the original footage and the work print.) The negative cutter finds the edge numbers and places the shots into the synchronizer with the edge numbers aligned side by side. Once the frames are lined up correctly, the editor will cut the original footage. The negative cut should be cement spliced.

ANSWER PRINT

When the negative cut has been completed, the *original* footage goes back to the lab for printing. At this point the footage will be "timed"—that is, a scene that looks too dark can be lightened or vice versa; one can even change skin tones somewhat. The lab makes a composite print, with picture and sound on a single strip of film, and all opticals such as titles and special effects included. The first print is usually called the "answer print" or "first trial print." If there are any changes or corrections to be made (preferably only minor ones), they should be taken care of now.

Once the answer print has been completed to your satisfaction, you are ready to have your "release prints" (the ones to be shown on theater screens) made. I suggest that you have a *"dupe"* made, leave the original safely tucked away in the vault, and have the release prints cut from the dupe.

8.

Equipment

Choosing the best (most effective) camera, lenses, raw stock, lights, and sound equipment is your camera director's privilege and responsibility. But you, the beginning director, should have at least some basic knowledge about the equipment to be used on your film. (I will never forget how embarrassed I was when during the shooting of my very first film, I confused a "Sennheiser" with a catering company.) So here we go. These are the areas we will discuss (hopefully in a short and painless way):

Cameras
Miscellaneous lenses
Sound equipment
Lights
Grip equipment

CAMERAS

The standard camera has been—and still is—the 35mm camera. You may choose among the Mitchell 35mm camera, the Mitchell Mark II S35R

HardFront camera, the Arriflex 35 BL camera (my choice), and the Arriflex Model II C/B camera. Generally these cameras should be rented with these accessories:

- *Mitchell 35mm:* Comes with 25mm, 35mm, 50mm, 75mm SuperLenses, two 1000' or four (better choice) 400' magazines, compact matte box, viewfinder, variable-speed or sync motor.
- *Mitchell Mark II S35R HardFront:* This camera is adapted for high speed and includes a 110-volt universal high-speed motor. It does not have support rods, required for zoom lenses, but has BNCT lens mounts and comes with 25mm, 50mm, and 75mm lenses, plus two 1000' magazines.
- *Arriflex 35 BL:* Self-blimped (camera noise does not interfere with sync sound), lightweight, can be hand-held. Includes 16mm, 24mm, 32mm, 50mm, 85mm Ziess F2 lenses, two 400' magazines, and crystal motor 24/25fps. Has dual-pin registration, matte box that accepts two 4" square filters plus one 3" square filter. Though expensive to rent, this is the very best if you are shooting sync sound.
- *Arriflex Model II C/B:* Has interchangeable 28mm, 50mm, 75mm Schneider lenses, two 400' or two 200' magazines, 16-volt variable-speed or constant speed motor, nicad battery. This camera will work well if you are on exterior location and do not have to shoot dialog.

There is a wide variety of excellent 16mm cameras on the market, but if you are shooting a feature film, I'd like to suggest that you choose a 35mm camera. Here is a list of the 16mm cameras:

- *Arriflex 16mm BL:* Comes with 12mm to 120mm zoom lens, matte box, universal motor or sync motor, one 400' magazine, and standard accessories, Eclair.
- *NPR or ACL 16mm:* Crystal universal motor, 16mm, 25mm, 50mm lenses, matte box, two 200' or one 400' magazine, nicad battery, and standard accessories.
- *Mitchell 16mm:* 17mm, 25mm, 35mm Baltar lenses, variable-speed motor, three 400' magazines, matte box, viewfinder and support bracket.
- *Frezzi Cordless Sound:* Crystal sync motor (for sync shooting), two

batteries (for dialog on location), charger, magnetic pickup head, two 400' magazines, 12 to 120mm zoom lens with finder. May be rented with sound equipment: MA-11 amplifier, microphone, and headset.
- *Bell & Howell 70R:* With 16mm, 25mm, 50mm lenses, one 400' magazine.
- *Bolex Rex:* With 16mm, 25mm, 75mm lenses. One 100' magazine.

If you are shooting on tape you need, of course, a video camera. During the past few years video cameras have come and gone, and you should consult a reliable rental outfit to decide which camera should be used. The cameras that have been used during the past few years are:

- *Ikegami HL-77, Ikegami HL-35:* Comes supplied with 10/100 Canon zoom lens, AC power supply, two batteries, battery charger, quick-release plate, output cables.
- *Hitachi FP-3030:* Comes supplied with zoom lens, battery, microphone, power supply/charger, output cables.
- *Sony DXC-1600 Trinicon:* Comes supplied with C.C.U. zoom lens, battery, power supply/charger, cables.

It is obvious that your choice of motion picture camera and accessories depends on the particular shots and/or scenes you have planned to film. (Note that whereas different motion picture cameras should be used for different parts of your motion picture, you will use the *same* video camera throughout your video project.) A dialog scene requires the expensive sync camera; an action scene calls for a hand-held camera that takes small (100' to 400') loads; if you wish to shoot the interior of a historical building that does not permit floodlights, you should select a camera that allows the shutter to be held open long enough for adequate exposure.

MISCELLANEOUS LENSES

Not all lenses adapt to all cameras. (Some 16mm cameras have permanently mounted lenses that are not interchangeable.) The interchangeable lenses are attached by a mechanism called the lens mount. As many as three lenses can be accommodated by the lens turret.

A variety of lenses unquestionably helps to make your footage exciting, since by using lenses of different focal length the camera director will produce various effects. There is such a variety of lenses on the market that we will discuss only the most commonly used ones.

The focal length of a normal lens is 35mm to 50mm. A telephoto lens has twice the focal length of the normal lens, and therefore the on-screen image will be twice the size of that obtained with a normal lens. Do not use a telephoto lens if you use a hand-held camera, as the image will jiggle. The telephoto lens will give you a shallow depth of field (the zone of sharp focus).

If you wish to give your audience a sense of perspective, your camera director chooses a wide-angle lens (lenses of different focal length do not have different perspectives). A wide-angle lens has a much greater depth of field than a normal lens, an important fact to consider when you shoot action, because with a wide-angle lens the camera director can shoot without having to follow focus during a shot. For instance, if you wish to create a dynamic impression of a fist coming toward the screen, use a wide-angle lens. The fist punching toward the audience will double in size.

The zoom lens can focus down to ⅜ of an inch in front of the subject. Shock zooms have been a standby (now already cliché) in horror pictures.

Viewfinder The camera director views what the camera sees through the viewfinder. The best system is a through-the-lens reflex viewfinder, in which the image transmitted through the lens is projected onto a ground glass. Always take into consideration the slight (but at times significant) difference between the image seen through the viewfinder and the image projected on the screen. This difference is called the parallax.

Camera Motors Motors are either spring wound or operated by an electric drive. You will find spring-wound motors on 16mm cameras only. Electrically driven motors do require a source of electric power or a battery. You'll find two types of electric motors: wild motors and synchronous motors. Wild motors permit various filming speeds. You are able to film at a faster speed than normal, and when the film is projected at normal speed the action on the screen will be slowed down. Conversely, if you film at a slower speed than normal, then project at normal speed, the action will speed up.

A synchronous motor is used as you shoot sync sound. On location this motor is run by battery power. To avoid unnecessary delays, ask your camera director to check the motor from time to time.

Variable Shutter Each frame is exposed by stopping briefly as it moves through the camera. The shutter blocks the light so that the film is exposed. Most likely your camera director will opt for a variable shutter. It can be shut down gradually, to effect a camera fadeout (you save on the expensive optical fadeout), and it allows the use of fast film for exterior shots, as well as a decreasing and/or increasing depth of field.

Filters Most cameras have a built-in filter for using indoor film outdoors, or they come equipped with a matte box that permits the use of gelatin filters in front of the lens. (Generally, however, if I may advise you, do *not* use outdoor raw stock for an indoor shot, and avoid indoor raw stock for an exterior shot.)

SOUND EQUIPMENT

The most flexible sound recorder is the Nagra. This recorder can be fitted with an oscillator identical to the unit that controls camera speed. The tape's running speed is recorded along the edge of the sound tape, thus giving a *precise* reference when picture and sound go into editing.

The starting point for sound and picture is marked by the *slate,* a board to which a piece of wood *(clapper)* has been hinged. The scene number, take number, production title, and name of director are penciled on the slate. Once the camera is up to speed, the production assistant holding the slate reads aloud the scene and take numbers, then slaps the clapper down on the board. Later on the editor will line up this banging noise with sound and picture tracks. The soundman should always wear earphones that are plugged into the Nagra, so he or she will be able to hear the sound exactly as it is picked up.

The best microphones on the market, as mentioned previously, are Sennheisers. At times you may want to use a *lavalier* mike, which can be attached to your actor's outfit. And, without any doubt, you need a *fishpole* mike, which dangles from a fishpolelike mechanism held above your actors.

The following is a basic sound package:

Nagra 4.2L Synchronous tape recorder, with three speeds,
    two OPSE-200 preamps, self-resolving camera speed

indicator, ATN unit, batteries, headset, soft and hard
    case.
Boom stand
Fishpole
Microphone desk stand
Sennheiser microphones
Microphone mixer

LIGHTS

Shooting your motion picture on film requires a fairly extensive light package:

Fresnels: Midget, Baby, Junior, Senior, Tener
Softlights
Arcs
Nooklights
Molettes
Minibrutes
Maxibrutes
    (all these come with silks, barn doors, and stands)
Overhead lights
Strip lights
Daylight source units—200, 400, 575, 2500 watts
    (stands, barn doors, gel frames, scrim net, snoot)
Mole Kit: Teenie mole kit, micky mole kit, mighty
    mole kit.

Needless to say, you do not need all these lights for every scene in your film. The light plot will change from location to location, and some changes may be needed between scenes and camera setups.

GRIP EQUIPMENT

And now, hold on to your seat as you take a look at the grip equipment necessary. I know it sounds like a lot, but please listen to me: it is better to have some equipment in store you'll never use, than to have to send a production assistant to fetch something. Delays are far more costly than a clamp that rents for a few dollars. So, here we go:

GRIP EQUIPMENT

Small sandbag
Large sandbag
⅛ apple box
¼ apple box
½ apple box
Full apple box
Flex arm (gooseneck)
Grip head and arm
C stand
Hi overhead stand w/wheels
Stair blocks (8)
Cup blocks (12)
Wedges (24)
Cribbing (24)
Clip boards (baby, junior, and senior)
12' × 12' butterfly set
6' × 6' butterfly set
4' × 4' silk
4' × 4' single net
4' × 4' double net
24" × 36" open end single
24" x 36" open end double
18" × 24" open end single
18" × 24" open end double
10" × 12" open end single or double
Dots: single, double, solid (set/6)
Fingers: single, double, solid (set/6)
5' × 4' solid flag
24" × 36" flag
18" × 24" flag
10" × 12" flag
24" × 36" open end silk
18" × 24" open end silk
24" × 72" cutter flag
18" × 48" cutter flag
10" × 42" cutter flag
4' × 4' cube

24″ × 36″ cube
18″ × 24″ cube
Alligator clamp
Ladders, 4′, 8′, 10′—each
Ladders, 12″ ext.—each
Umbrella and stand
6′ parallel and tops, w/wheel, post rails, and screen
    jacks
Bear claw
Meat ax
Furniture pad
Block and fall w/rope
Sawed off C-stand
Dolly track (4′ × 8′)
4′ × 4′ reflector (complete)
2′ × 2′ hand reflector (complete)
Ford axle
Auto tow bars
Grip box (complete with contents)
Double suction cups
Riser
Polecats
Bar clamp
12′ × 12′ tarp
20′ × 20′ tarp
20′ × 20′ black backing
20′ × 20′ white silk
20′ × 30′ white silk
Wall spreaders (2)
20′ × 20′ frame

MISCELLANEOUS

Director chair (high)
Director chair (regular)
Gold water cooler

Cooler box
Walkie-talkie set, batteries (5 watt)
Signal horn
Staple gun
Staples (as used)
Gas can w/spout
First-aid kit
Water hose
Nozzle
Broom
Dustpan
Garbage pail
Shovel
Posthole digger
Rake
Rubber mats, 24″ × 36″
Battery clip set
Flashlight

HANGERS AND MOUNTING ACCESSORIES

Baby offset arm
Furniture clamp (bar clamp), 12″ or 18″
Baby C-clamp ⅝ pin
Baby pipe clamp
Baby wall sled
Baby trombone
Baby nail-on plate (Reg. or 12″ Stud)
Baby boom
Gaffers grip
Junior Offset arm
Junior C-clamp
Junior pipe clamp
Junior wall sled
Junior trombone
Junior bazooka
Junior nail-on plate

Junior pigeon
Junior telescoping hanger, 6', 8', and 10'
Junior trapeze
Junior stand bracket
Junior set wall bracket
T-Bone (floor spider)
Senior wall sled

9.

Special Effects

Major production companies spend millions of dollars on breathtaking special effects. To be sure, these are not the ones to be discussed in this chapter. Instead we will cover those special effects that are within your budget and expertise. You will want to use these "homegrown" special effects if you:

Wish to avoid costly opticals.
Wish to avoid paying for expensive locations.
Need fire effects.
Need visually exciting shots that are either too
    expensive or too dangerous to shoot the
    conventional way.

Special Effects Instead of Opticals

"SUPER OVER" EFFECTS

Visually you want to convey your heroine's torn state of mind, so you have decided to superimpose her CU over a broken window. If you "super" the conventional way, that is, you first film the window, then the CU, then have the CU supered via opticals, you are facing a considerable expense.

Fortunately you'll achieve the same effect if you buy an inexpensive piece of glass, glue strips of plastic tape over it to resemble a broken window, place it in front of the camera, position your actress behind it, and—presto— shoot.

If you want a ghost to appear on-screen, you have two choices to avoid a costly optical:

• Coat a mirror slightly with petroleum jelly and film your actor's mirror image.

• Create a transparent ghost (only a little more complicated): choose a fairly dark environment in which (thanks to rim lighting) furniture and architectural details are only barely visible, and place a piece of window-sized glass in front of it. Position your actress (the ghost) some distance away from the glass, direct strong light beams on her, and film. Her image appearing on the screen will be frighteningly transparent.

"Now You See Me, Now You Don't" This great old standby is lots of fun to see on-screen, and easy to do. As you film your environment and actors, you'll have the camera stop at a *specific* moment. Make your ghost appear by positioning your actor in front of the camera. Then run the camera up to the moment when the ghost disappears. Stop the camera, remove the ghost, and complete the shot showing the actors who had been established previously. Easy to do if you keep in mind:

> The camera *must* be placed on a tripod. No hand-held
> camera for this specific effect.
> The actors present in the environment must freeze the
> moment the camera stops running.
> They must be in exactly the same positions when the
> camera starts rolling again.

Avoiding Expensive Locations

Dialog in Front of an Ancient Castle Given your budget, naturally you do not plan to travel to England to shoot the exterior of "Castle Hunsbury" but have to be satisfied with a stock shot of the edifice (many film libraries have a wide variety of magnificent stock shots). Have your art director paint some architectural detail on a piece of glass (glass image). Place the glass image in front of your camera and position your actors for a Medium Shot. The effect—your actors standing in front of a magnificent Renaissance window or within a heavily carved door frame—will be surprisingly real.

On the Train   Your script calls for a holdup on a vintage train. Naturally you won't find an old train that still runs; even if you did, the exorbitant rental fee would preclude filming on it. But you should be able (for some money, proof of insurance, and many, many good words) to film the interior of a nonmoving historical train. There are a number of train museums around, and many a small town has elevated its long-defunct train station to a local museum.

Film your actors boarding the train, making it a night shot if at all possible. Close the windowshades and light the lamps. With the shades closed, your audience won't be able to discern that the train is not moving. The actors must take care to rock to and fro in their seats, and the conductor and the holdup men must sway as they make their way through the aisle. All you need are the sounds of rumbling wheels and the rush of the steam engine, to be added during the editing process, and you have created a believable "on the train" scene.

On the Plane   You need not rent an expensive mockup of a plane interior. Rent only a few authentic plane seats (any motion picture prop house can supply them), have your art director build a mock window area, and every so often let a pretty stewardess walk by.

On the Bus   Shoot all your dialog scenes on a nonmoving bus. Later, place your actor on a moving bus and

> film the actor looking out of a window
> film the actor's POV.

Rain, Snow   You don't have to wait for rain or snow to hit your area before shooting an important exterior scene. Wet your actors' outfits, or sprinkle artificial snow on them. From your favorite supply house rent a rain or snow machine, have a production assistant hold it in front of the camera, and shoot.

Jungle and Forest Scenes   Jungle and forest scenes are easy to create. If you have a sufficient number of stock shots on hand for establishing shots, all you'll have to do is add the Medium and ¾ shots of your actors. For this purpose some very believable scenery can be created by covering a relatively small area with greenery. You can get any amount of greenery from a tree-trimming service, or—more expensive—rent it from a nursery.

Fire Effects

First of all, a word of warning: regardless of what your friends tell you, *never* attempt to do any effects requiring the use of flammables or gunpowder in-house. Neither you, the art director, nor any of your assistants is qualified for such tasks. Only a *certified* explosives expert (a motion picture supply house will have names available) should handle explosive and flammable materials.

Fire effects require the attendance of a fire marshal (you can get the names of retired firefighters from the municipal office that handles motion picture location permits), and a water truck and driver must be stationed at the location where the fire effect takes place. All these items run up your budget considerably. (The special effects for my film *Executioner II,* which showed Vietnam scenes including a helicopter, flamethrowers, and many extras, took up one-fourth the entire budget.) Because of the expense, think twice about whether your story really needs fire effects, and if so, whether a substitute effect might work just as well.

In one of my films the hero and heroine had to run through a burning building. The nature of our chosen location, a historical California mission, prevented even the thought of using real fire.

First we filmed a scale model of the mission's exterior with flames shooting out of windows and the roof. (Yes, we had an expert setting our model on fire, and yes, we will discuss scale models later.) In this way we established the burning mission in the audience's mind.

For the interior shot, our gaffer mounted red gels over all production lights. A pan of dry ice in hot water was held in front of the camera. (A smoke machine from a motion picture rental house would have been better, but because of the artifacts in the building, smoke could not be used.) Finally, production assistants waved blankets in front of the lamps as our actors ran "through the fire" to safety.

Extraordinary Visual Effects

(Miniatures)

Miniatures are your answer if you need extraordinary visual effects that are either too dangerous or too expensive to shoot the conventional way. Most art directors are enthusiastic creators of miniatures. They create great-looking stuff from practically nothing. If you desire top-quality miniatures, you may commission a special effects studio. Major production companies use miniatures all the time. The fantastic sea-air battle scenes we admired in the film *Tora! Tora! Tora!* were created using miniatures. The term *miniatures,* agreed, seems to be somewhat misleading when one considers that the battleships used for *Tora! Tora! Tora!* were each about eighteen feet long. Don't worry—the miniatures we are talking about are on a more conservative scale.

A CAR GOES OVER A CLIFF

If you should consider the conventional way of shooting a car going over a cliff, you have to count on a full shooting day on a remote location that features a road and cliffs, a special permit, a fire marshal plus water truck and driver, possibly a motorized police escort, a stunt car rigged for the stunt (expensive), a skilled stunt driver, a tow car and team to pull the totaled car up from the cliff, a junkyard that will take the car, and last but not least a *huge* insurance policy. (Believe me, a shot that lasts a few seconds on the screen takes all of this—I have done it.)

You may, of course, buy a stock shot of a car going over a cliff, which is fine if just any type of car will do. If, as is most likely, the car going over the cliff had been established as an important part of your story, you better have a miniature made. This miniature car going over a miniature cliff must resemble the actual car used in previous scenes in color, shape, and detail as closely as possible, or you'll be in trouble.

The effect works as follows: Your stunt driver drives the actual car to the spot where it is supposed to go over the cliff (the dangerous promontory ought to be comfortably far away), then by way of clever editing you cut to the shot of the miniature car going over the cliff.

In shooting miniatures, remember that the audience should see the miniature for *short* periods of time only. Therefore, *intercut* the miniature's action with a number of shots of the driver's face, her hands on the steering wheel, hands covering her face, etc.

Also, don't forget that you must show the actual time it would take the actual car to go over the cliff, which is another reason why you intercut with the driver's reactions.

A YACHT EXPLODES

Let's assume that part of your film takes place on a yacht that—at the film's climax—explodes. Cleverly you have scheduled the explosion to occur at night. All action and dialog are to be filmed on the "actual location," the yacht you have rented for that purpose. As tempting as it may be, do *not* take the yacht out to the open sea when filming. Leave it safely anchored in the harbor, if you want to avoid unattractive back-and-forth rocking during framing. Take the yacht out for the Establishing and POV shots only.

The climax, after your characters have made their way to a life raft, is indeed the explosion. Remember it is night—a moonless night—so the miniature needs to resemble the actual yacht in outline only. Your art director has built a believable ocean by using nothing more expensive or elaborate than dark green plastic garden bags. Behind the ocean is placed the *cyclorama* (a slightly curved background) of the dark night sky. A dark fishing line is attached to the miniature yacht and slowly, while the camera rolls, a steady-handed production assistant pulls the yacht across the plastic ocean.

For the ensuing explosion (I have to remind you) you have to hire an explosives expert, unless you wish to face the possibility of the studio's going up in flames.

Getting back to the scene as your characters evacuate the yacht: By now, to be realistic, the sinking yacht ought to be in a tilted position, which, because of the sheer weight of the craft, cannot be done safely. A smaller boat has to be substituted for the yacht. Have your production manager look for a small-craft dry dock. Rent a boat that has been placed on a wooden frame for repairs. Shooting at night, fasten a tarpaulin behind the boat and tilt the boat slightly. Do *not* allow your production assistants or grips to do this job, but leave it up to the dry dock's employees—they know how to handle boats safely. Set up for a ¾ Shot, to be intercut with CUs and Medium Shots, and shoot your characters evacuating the craft.

A UFO CRASHES IN THE BACKYARD

Don't despair if your script calls for a UFO crash, but put in a call to your art director. Calmly she will inform you that the special effect requires two easy-to-come-by items: a UFO miniature, and a glass image.

The art director will create the UFO miniature, which has to be placed against a sky background. If you have wisely chosen a night scene, flickering Christmas lights on the UFO will add a feeling of reality. For a daytime shoot you might want to use dry ice to give cloud effects. Two fishing lines have to be attached to the UFO. The rigging of the second is somewhat tricky, as this is the line that directs the UFO's descent.

With the limited resources at your disposal, you cannot film the UFO's actual crash, but will have to find other means to make this scene believable. So, you show the interior of a suburban house (most likely the people living there will play an important part in your story anyway), and have your characters *hear* all the terrifying sounds that accompany the UFO's crash.

Next you show the crashed UFO—no big deal to that. Your art director has painted a glass image of it, which will be mounted in front of the camera in such a way that it seems the UFO barely missed the house.

A Moving Train   A moving train is easy to film. Depending on the kind of train you need, many types of train models, including surrounding environment, will do. To create a truly believable effect, you ought to film the moving train via an *aerial* shot; your camera director, with a hand-held camera, perches on the top rung of a ladder while shooting.

The Burning City   This effect also needs to be shot from an elevated camera position. From cardboard boxes, barrels, some magazine cutouts, and strings of Christmas lights, your art director has created a nighttime (forget about daytime) urban street. Most likely the miniature set is about two feet high and eight to ten feet long. May I remind you that a miniature, in order to look real, can be shown only briefly, so you must intercut with exterior nighttime shots of an actual urban street and interior shots of the cars whose occupants are involved in the story. For the fire effect, let me repeat, you will hire an explosives expert.

I hope these few examples have given you a taste for creating your own homegrown special effects. They are lots of fun to do.

Safety with Guns

Permit me to say a few words about the use of guns on the set. I know, every action film requires at least one good shoot-out. Fine. But guns, even the blanks that are used, are dangerous. Don't forget, *blanks can kill.* Some producers insist on using blanks because a small wisp of smoke escapes the barrel at the moment the gun is fired. If you have to use blanks, please observe the following safety rules:

- Do not permit actors or crew to "horse around" with the guns.
- Assign a responsible "gun handler" to hand out guns before every scene using them, and to collect the guns after the scene finishes.
- Allow only the gun handler to load the guns, and make him or her responsible for the blanks used.
- Do not permit any loaded guns in a scene that does not require a shoot-out. For these scenes, have the gun handler check *each* gun to see whether it is loaded.

On the films I produce, I must admit, I do not permit the use of blanks. I prefer to rent guns that cannot be loaded because the barrel has been blocked. True, no little wisp of smoke escapes while our hero or villain fires the gun, but so far I have not received any complaints. Besides, no matter which type of gun one uses, gunshot sounds have to be added later in the mix, because blanks do not sound quite genuine.

Well, we've come to the end of this book. I hope my advice and suggestions will help you get a project of your own off the ground. Good luck.

. . . .

Suggested Reading

Bare, Richard L. *The Film Director*. New York: Collier Books, 1971.

Harmon, Renée. *Film Producing: Low-Budget Films That Sell*. Hollywood, Calif.: Samuel French Trade, 1989.

———. *How to Audition for Movies and TV*. New York: Walker and Company, 1992.

Seger, Linda. *Making a Good Script Great*. Hollywood, Calif.: Samuel French Trade, 1987.

Index